THE GRAPHIC DESIGNER'S GUIDE TO CREATIVE MARKETING

THE

GRAPHIC DESIGNER'S GUIDE TO CREATIVE MARKETING

Finding & Keeping Your Best Clients

Linda Cooper Bowen

John Wiley & Sons, Inc.

New York · Chichester · Weinheim · Brisbane · Singapore · Toronto

This publication is designed to provide accurate and authoritative information in regard to the subject matter covered. It is sold with the understanding that the publisher is not engaged in rendering professional services. If professional advice or other expert assistance is required, the servicesof a competent professional person should be sought.

Library of Congress Cataloging-in-Publication Data:

Bowen, Linda Cooper.

The graphic designer's guide to creative marketing : finding and

keeping your best clients / Linda Cooper Bowen.

p.   cm.

Includes index.

ISBN 0-471-29314-0 (cloth : alk. paper)

1. Commercial art—United States—Marketing.   I. Title.1

NC1001.6.B68   1999

741.6' 068'8—dc21   98-35011

Printed in the United States of America.

10 9 8 7 6 5 4 3 2 1

To my father,
Ted Flato
The apple doesn't fall far from the tree
June 1998

CONTENTS

ACKNOWLEDGMENTS

Grateful acknowledgement is made to the following for permission to reprint excerpts from my previously published material: "Is Anyone Listening?" *I.D.* Magazine, Jan./Feb.1997; "Designing a Lifestyle" *Communication Arts*, May/June 1997; "The Thinking Designer: Moving Out of the Box," *AIGA Journal*, 1997 Vol. 15; "How To Profit From a Reality Check," *Graphis*, Jan./Feb. 1997.

The use of case studies, interviews and examples of self-promotional design has greatly contributed to the vitality of of this book. I am grateful for the cooperation and interest of the following designers, clients, educators and significant leaders in the design profession:
Sean Adams, Noreen Morioka, AdamsMorioka
Curt Altmann, Storm
Robert Anders, Pratt Institute of Art & Design
David Baker, ReCourses
William Bevington, Parsons School of Design
Jack Biesek, Biesek Design Associates
Michael Boland, Watts Design?
Sabra Brock, The Learning Partnership
Peggy Burke, 1185 Design
AnneLouise Burns, Blue Sky Design Company
Ilise Benum, The Art of Self Promotion
Ken Carbone, Leslie Smolan, Carbone Smolan Associates
Sheree Clark, Sayles Graphic Design

Michael Cohen, Peter Godefroy, Cohen Godefroy Design

Christine Costello, Art Technology Group

Steven DePuis, The DePuis Group

Kenneth DeLor, The DeLor Group

Sarah DeFillipis, Williams and House

Bill Ferguson, INC Design

Ric Grefé, Director, AIGA

Sonia Gretman, Gretman Design Group

Roz Goldfarb

Sarah J. Hall, SJH Design + Studio

Peter Hall, I.D. Magazine

Laurel Harper

John Haskitt, Illinois Institute of Design

Steven Heller

Caroline Hightower

Christie Lambert Rasmussen, Lambert Design

Jim Ludwigs, Ernst & Young

Janet Martin, Communication Arts, Inc.

Michael McGinn, Designframe

James Murray, Federated Merchandising Group

Mark Oliver, Mark Oliver Design

Kurt and Denise Palmquist, Palmquist & Palmquist Design

Rod Parker, DSI/LA

Victoria Peslak, Platinum Design

Wendy Peters, Gary Underhill, UP Design

Maria Ruotolo

Robert Ruttenberg, Gryphon Development Inc.

Linda Blount-Strauss, Benton Oil & Gas Inc.

Susan Slover, Slover and Company

Anne Telford, Communication Arts Magazine

Beth Tondreau, BTD Design

Pamela Vassil, Parsons School of Design

Petrula Vrontikis, Vrontikis Design Office

Brian Werling, Vaughn Wedeen Creative Inc.

Hunter Wimmer, NEO Design

INTRODUCTION

The inspiration for this book came as a result of teaching a few marketing seminars at the University of California at Santa Barbara and Parsons School of Design in New York. Making a reading list of books on the subject, I realized that there was no single book that covered marketing and account management for designers, showed samples of successful self-promotions and discussed how to prepare for the future by continuing their education.

When I started my first job as an account executive, following a 12-year career as a graphic designer, a book like this certainly would have been welcome. Although I knew about design from the creative side, I did not learn about how to find and keep new business until I started selling. Fortunately, I come from a long line of salesmen; perhaps there is a genetic proclivity for this profession. In any case I began a new career in design marketing and have found it to be especially creative and rewarding. Everything I have learned working as a graphic designer, account executive and marketing consultant has contributed to this book. In fact, during the course of my research I have talked to dozens of savvy designers and marketing educators, and I know more now than I did when this project began a year ago. I'm continually discovering something new and interesting.

I have approached this book, as I approach a new class or client, without any preconceived assumptions, a clean slate. The tone is conversational, informal, and I hope, enjoyable to read. A young graphic designer and early reviewer, referred to my "kick-butt" style, saying that she felt I was talking directly to her and found the book highly motivating. This is exactly what I wanted to hear; if I can have such a positive impact on many more readers I will be gratified. It has taken me many years to acquire this wisdom and I am happy to share it with designers who have, or plan to have, their own firms, as well as account people who are responsible for finding new business and maintaining client relationships.

Special appreciation goes to my friend and unofficial editor, Caroline Hightower, who generously offered her time, wisdom, and moral support. This project was undertaken thanks to my husband, Sava Mitrovich, whose love and nourishment made it possible.

THE GRAPHIC DESIGNER'S GUIDE TO CREATIVE MARKETING

1

WHAT IS MARKETING?

Since it can take about 50 cold calls to generate one new job, every design firm must establish its own efficient business development strategy—a systematic way of finding and keeping clients—in order to be a healthy, growing enterprise. The design business is changing and with increased competition for work, designers have to be more aggressive and inventive than ever before. The basic objective of marketing is simply to get and keep a customer. As a concept, marketing is quite straightforward, and in practice, a surprisingly fresh and enjoyable activity. Unfortunately, many designers, with only an art school education, have a negative re-action to what seems to be a boring, non-artistic effort that dis-tracts them from aesthetic concerns and the daily servicing of clients. Marketing reminds them that they are in a business, not a fine art, and must respond to the demands of customers with their own needs and ideas. This is reality.

SELLING AND MARKETING

Designers often confuse "selling" with "marketing." The distinction between the two is that selling often refers only to the offering of goods or services, and marketing involves creating a focused plan to locate and contact specific prospects. Theodore Levitt, the Harvard Business School's "guru of marketing," describes the difference succinctly: "Selling focuses on the needs of the seller, marketing on the needs of the buyer." Perhaps part of the problem is our association of selling with a slick, high-pressure technique to make you buy goods or services that you do not need or want. This is an unfair stereotype. We all buy, and we all sell, even ideas, and when marketing is done with imagination and intelligence, the service is appreciated. Respect it— it works.

Selling an intangible service like design involves special considerations. You do not manufacture a product that can be sampled, tried on or tasted, and although you can show examples of work produced for other companies, the prospective client is, with good reason, apprehensive about hiring you. In addition to your design ability, your business acumen, ethics and ability to communicate effectively will be tested, and you must deliver on what you promise. If you are a freelance designer it's time to start thinking of yourself as a small business or design studio and learn to understand the basics of financials, payables, receivables, regulations and taxes. Find a good accountant, business manager and lawyer and with their help, master the mechanics of operating as a business. When you begin to relate to the bottom-line considerations of your own company, you will be better at understanding how your client looks at things, giving you an invaluable perspective.

Selling focuses on the needs of the seller, marketing on the needs of the buyer.
Theodore Levitt

WHO NEEDS MARKETING ?

Marketing is as important to the seasoned professional as it is for the young designer setting up a new practice. A basic marketing plan is key to identifying the clients you most want to work with and provides a concrete program to attract and keep them. It is surprising to me how many firms are "flying blind," living from one job to the next, never sure when or where the next client will come from. Like the equally requisite business plan, the marketing program offers a map of where you want to go and how to get there. The process of creating this on your own or with an experienced marketing consultant will clarify your immediate and long-range goals, identify problems and weaknesses, give your self-confidence a boost and help to build a effective system of locating the best, most profitable projects. The objective here is not only financial success but creative fulfillment and the satisfaction of knowing that you have a certain amount of control over your life.

GETTING STARTED

I recently spoke to a young designer about how she markets herself. Her comments sounded typical of talented people who just haven't made the time or created a budget to seriously pursue new business in a professional manner. She has just enough work to be busy but not enough to feel secure. The fact that she has clients despite zero promotion effort tells me that she must have talent, but, as she admitted, "I know I should be doing the same kind of communication I advise my clients to do, but I just can't face it." This comment revealed an inability to apply her knowledge of creative, economical design and production to her own business, as well as a sensitive, rather shaky ego. My advice to her was to just get started, even on a modest level, then build her way up to a real program. If you won't invest in your own business, then what's the point?

It is a common dilemma . . . either a designer is too busy to devote time to marketing and doesn't think about it until there is no work in the office, or when there is a financial crunch, he is too concerned about cost to make the investment. Paralyzed by the shortage of time or money, the designer takes no action, passively waiting for the phone to ring, or as they say, "for work to come in over the transom." When is the last time you saw a transom? What is a transom, anyway?

MARKETING AS A TOOL

A more positive message comes from Mark Oliver, principal, Mark Oliver, Inc. in Santa Barbara, California. "In the service sector," (I like that—he is not embarrassed to admit that graphic design is a service), "marketing is a tool for creating and building relationships. It is important to remember that business relationships are closely tied to personal relationships. The contact you make each time you reach a prospect is with a human being with whom a both personal and business relationship will hopefully be built. The more times contact is made with that person, the more they will be likely to remember you for the next available project. Marketing forces us to focus on questions like, 'What makes us special?' 'What is our unique selling proposition?' 'Why should someone choose to work with us?' and 'How can we improve the product?' We think of marketing as a tool for creating and building relationships. The process can take as long as two years, and consumes staff time and money, but we have learned that persistence pays and timing is everything."

The first constructive move you have to make is to radically change your attitude. Rather than facing the marketing of your design services as a tiresome chore akin to balancing your checkbook, think of it as a game. The fact is, marketing is not an op-

We have learned that persistence pays and timing is everything.

Mark Oliver

tion, it is a necessity . . . but it can also be fun. After a series of goals have been identified, such as a database tracking system, targeted prospect list, and new self-promotion material, you are now free to reach the objective in the most imaginative way you can. This may not always be accomplished solely as a graphic design solution, but often in bold, playful ways as a result of good research and timely action.

MEMORABLE COMMUNICATIONS

When I was an account executive I read that a client of ours had just acquired a chain of fast-food hamburger outlets. Anticipating that this could possibly mean a new identity for the acquired company, I wanted to put our name in front of him in a way that would get his attention. I found a cleverly packaged set of beanbags shaped like a hamburger, which I had hand-delivered with this message on lettuce-green paper: "Congratulations! XX Design would RELISH working with you and your new company." Did we get that job? To be honest, no, there was no opportunity for redesign at that time, but we definitely made an impression as an informed, witty office, and later that year we were called in to do an extensive identity project for another division of the corporation. At the risk of being perceived as corny or overly aggressive, it paid off. Even faxes can be creative. I once made a laser print of the fortune from a cookie saved from lunch at a nearby Chinese restaurant because I thought the "fortune" might be appropriate sometime. When I found the right occasion, I faxed it to a client, and got an immediate, pleased response. Appropriate, amusing messages on voice mail, or clever E-mail notes will make your communications memorable, and in our super-high-tech world, these personal, human touches are especially appreciated.

THE CLIENT IS YOU

Designers pride themselves on their ability to work with a wide variety of clients on many kinds of projects, finally arriving at the distinctive graphic solution that will result in more sales of the product or service. Doing this for a client is relatively easy because you can be objective. However, analyzing your own business as a marketing problem is difficult because it is inevitably self-critical. With the prospect of selling your own creative services, you are forced to take the part of the client as you examine your case for what makes your office so special. This process should be considered a worthwhile opportunity to take an objective assessment of your practice, set goals and watch the program ultimately succeed . . . and it is also creatively satisfying.

I asked Hunter Wimmer, principal of NEO Design in Washington, D.C., whether he considered marketing enjoyable or a chore. He said, "Enjoyable. We know ourselves better than we know any of our clients, so the task at hand is more personal and the end results are far more rewarding. Without good marketing, good design can go unnoticed. It's the most direct way to ensure future visibility and success." The structure of a plan is simple, yet each design firm has its own distinct personality, a particular point of view about life in general and especially graphic design, that makes it unique. Every marketing program is an expression of this challenge and pleasure. It is an exercise that makes you smarter and more aware of the business and life of the designer.

Without good marketing, good design can go unnoticed.
Hunter Wimmer,
NEO Design

MARKETING "OUT THERE"

Last year I wrote an article for *Communication Arts Magazine* entitled, "Designing a Lifestyle," which was inspired by my own curiosity about designers who live and work in the less obvious metropolitan locations like Louisville, Kentucky; Baton Rouge,

Louisiana; or more rustic places like San Luis Obispo, California and Bozeman, Montana. If marketing design services is tough in New York or Los Angeles, what might it be like out there? The answers I got to these and other questions were thoughtful and wise.

Louisville, Kentucky

Ken DeLor, president of The DeLor Group in Louisville, Kentucky, has been in business for 15 years and has grown from a small freelance studio to a 27-person office in his own historic building on Main Street. "Nearly all of our clients are located in other parts of the country. Our online capabilities are useful in maintaining close communication with them and in facilitating project flow. And we frequently go online to conduct research. We promote our services on a national level to strategic players in the specific industries in which we have a lot of experience, particularly pharmaceuticals and industrial manufacturing. Two full-time business development people are dedicated to this mission. Our promotional efforts include direct mail to targeted prospects and a quarterly newsletter containing information on branding and pertinent market trends. We also work with a consultant to support our public relations campaign." How does Ken stay stimulated and keep the work fresh and relevant? "We rely on the diversity of the work itself. The complex issues our clients face present us with challenges beyond design needs, and hiring the best young designers brings imagination and freshness to what we do. New York is a vibrant, exciting city, but it's also a complicated, expensive place. You can get emotionally drained there and easily turn cynical. Louisville, on the other hand, tends to be the epitome of Southern hospitality. The climate is mild, cost of living is low and the arts are heavily supported by the business community. Once we get someone down here they never want to leave."

San Luis Obispo, California

When I asked Jack Biesek of Biesek Design Associates, an environmental graphics design firm in San Luis Obispo, California, about the drawbacks and advantages of having a home-based office far from a major city, he explained, "The advantages outweigh the disadvantages, since quality of life is most important to me. We feel fortunate to live amongst the oak trees and chaparral in a canyon not far from the Pacific Ocean, and yet are able to work with clients in the real world (metropolitan areas). The profile I have developed for a good client includes nice people, appropriate budget and an interesting project. If I can't hit on two of these criteria . . . I won't accept the work. Life is too short to settle for less, and there is plenty of work to choose from." Jack sees himself as actively choosing from, rather than being chosen by, prospective clients—what a refreshingly healthy attitude. "I have a fairly assertive approach to marketing . . . I look for the type of work I want to do and find it. It's a simple equation . . . a numbers game really . . . based on numerical odds, random selection, communication skills, human chemistry and perceived needs (i.e. vision) of the client. Oh, and don't forget luck. Computers are rapidly changing the way we do business, as in 'super-targeting' and 'micro-marketing.' These two buzzwords mean the ability to find exactly the kind of work my firm desires: quality projects with adequate budgets from clients who understand and appreciate professional services.

I've learned that by specializing, it is much easier to find work. Of the last 25 major jobs I've gotten . . . 90% of those jobs came from being the most qualified. Most of the work was only bid by our firm and in competitive bidding we were selected over other firms that offered lower fees. We know our business and deliver genuine value at a fair price. Our clients recognize this and our experience is one of our biggest assets. Word-of-mouth referrals have worked well for us; we're getting to be known as 'the sign guys' and our clients are entrusting us with bigger and more compre-

The profile I have developed for a good client includes nice people, appropriate budget and an interesting project.

Jack Biesek

hensive projects. Finding new clients is an aspect of the business I find enjoyable and rewarding."

Bozeman, Montana

Palmquist & Palmquist Design in Bozeman, Montana is a husband-and-wife partnership that was started six years ago after the two decided to move back home after beginning their design careers in the big city of Seattle. Not finding any full-time jobs in their field, they were forced to set up their own shop in order to stay in Montana. "Some people told us the only way we were going to work here was to start drawing cowboy boots and cows, but we've been fortunate enough to be able to make a living, start a family and enjoy the beauty of living in this area.

Our client base is everything from bed and breakfasts to high-tech industries and outdoor products manufacturers. Many of them have moved existing businesses from other parts of the country to Bozeman, and their markets are national and international. Our clients have found that they can live here and still be in touch with the rest of the world. It has been a tough road for us because budgets are smaller here, and the market is less educated about the cost and benefits of good design. Although we are considered expensive locally, we aren't getting close to what we should.

We work hard to make a living and are constantly trying to find the best way to market to larger companies outside of the region. It's important to let people know that we choose to live here and that Palmquist & Palmquist is just as creative here as we would be in a larger city. Whenever we find ourselves questioning the wisdom of what we're doing here, we take a short drive to the Madison River on a summer evening to do some fly fishing. Standing there in the river, we realize that there is more to life than what colors to use on a particular job, or that earlier hassle with the printer."

Some people told us the only way we were going to work here was to start drawing cowboy boots and cows.
Kurt Palmquist

THE NEW YORK CITY APPROACH

At the opposite side of the country is New York City, with the most dense concentration of both design firms and prospective clients. There is no shortage here of creative stimulation, unlimited cultural opportunities and a tempo of life that provides a daily supplement of high energy. How can a design firm of any size define itself in this extremely competitive market, find good clients and enjoy the benefits of super-urban life? By making a marketing plan and being disciplined enough to follow through and use it.

Bill Ferguson, one of the three founding principals of INC Design, a corporate design firm specializing in annual reports, capabilities brochures and identity programs, reminds us that you can have a program and still make changes. "Our marketing program is formalized at the beginning of each calendar and modified throughout the year, depending upon company developments and/or market circumstances, issues or needs that arise. Situations unforeseen in January may dictate a new approach in our program by June. Spontaneity can be fun, but we clearly prefer a well thought out plan. We think through ways to realize our goals, and develop innovative, practical tools to get us the desired result—new business. These tools include promotional mailings, educational seminars, telemarketing programs, surveys, press releases and organizational memberships, all of which are part of our plan to build awareness of our work and presence in the business community, and ignite the interest of a prospective customer who will hopefully agree to a personal meeting or presentation."

For Victoria Peslak, whose firm, Platinum Design, has succeeded in maintaining a growing list of highly visible clients, working in New York City is a different marketing situation. "Marketing is important to the success of my company because it substantiates us as an important company and creates an opportunity to show our professionalism and track record. The program keeps us fresh in the client's mind. You have to hustle harder here."

What particularly impresses me about the passionate believers in marketing is not only the fact that they really understand its theory and practice, but they also take keen pleasure in the sport aspect of marketing. One successful design firm principal always rewards himself after bringing in a prized new account by buying himself a Hermes tie. His ties are like trophies, each reminding him of a particularly special "win."

MARKETING IS A STATE OF MIND

Marketing becomes an ongoing state of mind, an instinctive act, a reflex. You read a magazine article about a new company or hear something at a business meeting that sounds like an opportunity and you respond automatically. At once, you find the contact name, address and telephone number of the company and add it to your database, then you decide what the best approach will be. People who do this well seem to just "get it"—they are naturals—but it is also possible to learn good marketing skills. Skeptical or reluctant designers become enthusiastic converts when they see their efforts pay off.

THE MARKETING PLAN OUTLINE

The following outline represents a plan of action to develop new business. It can be simple or complex. The important thing is to create a marketing plan you will actually use. The process of analysis will give you a clear picture of what defines you as a firm and where you want to go. Setting goals gives you a sense of control and offers the great satisfaction of seeing the plan work. Review it at least quarterly, and update or revise it as necessary.

RESEARCH

1. Internal Survey

a. Review Portfolio: Study client and types of projects (size, location and profitability)

b. Goals: Write a statement of personal and professional goals and values

c. Assess Capabilities: Define your firm's special qualifications and abilities

2. External Survey

a. In a formal or informal survey, identify strengths and weaknesses of your work and staff

b. Analyze the competition by reading design trade magazines and asking consultants, vendors

c. Study market trends, new technologies, media

3. Target Your Market

Select your new clients based on the following;

a. Type of project or industry, demand

b. Capabilities, present and future

c. Interest in project or industry

Strategy

1. Goals

a. Describe your firm's desired goals, state measurable financial objectives

2. Positioning

a. Define the image of your firm, personal style, what
   makes your office unique?

b. Specify the targeted markets you want to work with

c. List the services you will offer to these markets

d. Define your geographic range

3. Tactical Action Plan

a. List necessary actions to win new projects and
   clients in targeted market, including additional staff
   and equipment, budget required

b. Visibility
   Describe activities that will create a higher visibility of
   your work and firm

Implementation

1. Self-Promotion Program

a. Establish database/mailing list

b. Identify objectives, necessary project elements
   (i.e. brochure, newsletter, press release, speeches,
   articles)

c. Establish budget

d. Create marketing schedule/calendar

(see example, Chapter 5)

THE ROLE OF THE MARKETING ACCOUNT MANAGER/RAINMAKER:
or How to Do it Yourself

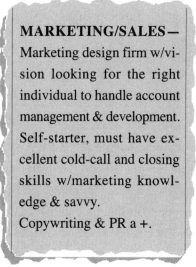

MARKETING/SALES—
Marketing design firm w/vision looking for the right individual to handle account management & development. Self-starter, must have excellent cold-call and closing skills w/marketing knowledge & savvy.
Copywriting & PR a +.

WHAT IT TAKES

To be successful in this job, an individual needs a combination of intelligence, salesmanship, perseverance and a sense of humor. First, as in selling any product or service, you have to know your company's capabilities, the competition and the market. Be prepared. If you are not totally sure about any of this, be willing to take the time to learn this information before you go out and present the firm's work. You will probably get only one chance to see this prospective client; don't waste it. If you exhibit ignorance or uncertainty, it makes you and your firm seem unprofessional and unworthy of serious consideration.

As the representative of the design office you must impress the prospect not only with the portfolio, but also with your ability to listen. In that first meeting especially, spend more time listening than talking. Your goal is not to be considered as a "vendor" but a partner . . . a creative collaborator. Don't expect to "get an order" after one presentation. This process can be long and slow, so if you are not willing to persevere, sometimes for years, this job is not for you. As the outside person, you must win business not only on the quality of the design portfolio, but on your strategic marketing skills and talent for creating lasting business relationships.

DO IT YOURSELF

If you, the designer, are acting as your own marketing/sales person you have some obvious advantages; there is no marketing individual to share the fees with, the prospect can deal directly with the creative firm's principal and you know the history of every job, including the problems solved, client profiles and the costs. Hopefully you are also an engaging, articulate speaker, an effective salesperson and are able to negotiate and close the deal successfully. If this is not the case you should either spend the time to learn how become better in these areas or consider taking on a partner who already has these talents. Realize that marketing can take a lot of your time, so if you are unable to devote many hours away from the demands of current projects and client issues, hire an experienced marketing professional to do it right.

Engaging an eager but inexperienced candidate for the job means you can expect a long orientation (training) period which may or may not result in getting any significant new business. It is a rather recent development for design firms to have people in the marketing role, but this is now a viable career option for someone with advertising sales experience or a background in public relations, possibly client-side training or even a lapsed graphic designer like myself. I would not hesitate to recommend this as an excellent job for a design school graduate with a few years experience working for a design office. An intelligent marketing executive has the ability to track, bring in and manage new clients, as well as contribute an objective view of how to grow the company. In the future, the marketing and sales executive will be universally accepted as an integral, necessary member of the design business and I am optimistic about the opportunities in this area for young people with intelligence, discipline and initiative.

JOB DESCRIPTION

Before running an ad or contacting a headhunter, it is necessary to define what the duties and responsibilities of this position involve. Why do you need this person? What will they do—generate new business leads, make presentations, write proposals? Will they be involved as an account liaison throughout the project or not? What additional duties, like copywriting, will be expected? What kind of clerical support do you offer, or will they be doing a lot of word-processing and data entry on their own? How will they be compensated—salary, commission plus salary, or a partnership arrangement? You should have answers to these questions before the hiring process starts, because you both need to be very clear about these expectations at the outset. Write down, for your own reference, as well as that the new hire, the duties of the job. Although the job titles define responsibilities, there can be some overlap. Individual firms have their own particular needs depending on size and organizational style.

Account Services Manager, Account Executive:

Work directly with client as liaison between creative staff, write letters, proposals, oversee budget, sometimes assist in new business development. Considered a middle or senior management salaried position.

Marketing Executive, Director, New Business Development:

Sole responsibility for new business, employing skills in telemarketing, research, sales presentations. May also continue as liaison between client and creative staff, and write press releases, proposals, letters. Compensation generally on a commission plus salary basis, or draw against commission.

A HEADHUNTER'S VIEW

Roz Goldfarb, the New York-based headhunter, describes the personal characteristics that make someone successful in this job: "It's a balance between intelligence and savvy, innate understanding and life experience, plus training. There has to be an intuitive sense of what makes something click. The ability to move a design services business forward requires skills in understanding, analyzing and interpreting information. This person has to be able to develop a strategy, a vision, to propel a design firm into the business climate, and it requires a lot of creative thinking. They have to be problem-solvers with the ability to read between the lines. The most successful account executives are charming, polite people with a sense of humor; you enjoy being with them. Marketing and account people have a talent for persuading as well as listening. They have to have a hunger for it, and think of marketing as a sport. Those individuals who find it fun see it as a challenge and will be deterred by nothing. For those not as self-assured, the prospect of facing rejection is too discouraging.

Savvy salespeople are unflappable. They see the "big picture" and don't take rejection personally. The history of design firms has changed. It's not enough just to hang out a shingle. Firms are now positioning themselves as marketing communications consultants, providing consultant services as well as graphic design. These larger offices now work on targeting, branding, identity and positioning projects that may sometimes not involve design at all. In these firms there are more "suits" than designers. Smaller companies cannot offer this, so their marketing person must position them in this client environment. The future outlook for the design marketing professional is very strong and presents tremendous opportunities as a viable career."

THE IN-HOUSE MARKETING SYSTEM

Most offices have no more than one individual responsible for new business development. In a medium-sized or even large firm, the office will provide clerical support for mailings and special projects, but very often the marketing person will be doing everything, including letters, data entry, and mailings himself.

The marketing department should be a separate office or quiet area that includes a library of work samples, slides and or CD-ROMs, research and reference books, presentation folders and the firm's capabilities brochure and self-promotion kit. The image of a salesperson happily running out the door with a slick presentation for the big corporate meeting is the result of many hours of planning and preparation.

Savvy salespeople are unflappable. They see the "big picture" and don't take rejection personally.
Roz Goldfarb

THE OFFICE WITHIN THE OFFICE

In my own marketing career, I found that I operated like an independent business within the design office. Without a specific directive from the boss other than to bring in good clients, how I accomplished this goal was my own creative responsibility, and yes, I do find this kind of work very creative.

Unlike the rest of the staff, who are working on jobs already in house, the sales and marketing member of the team is focused towards the future, on new prospects, opportunities and goals. In order to make the best use of the time in the office, a disciplined system of promotional literature has to be established so that leads can be responded to quickly and professionally. This includes a response-to-inquiry cover letter, meeting follow-up thank you, brochure or sample packet, press release format, client list, biography/mission statement, reference letters, and a supply of work samples from the past two or three years. It is smart to pay for a few hundred of the firm's best projects while they are being printed; don't expect the client to give these to you. It is also important to take slides and photographs of the work on a regular basis for presentations, publication and competition entries. Plan ahead.

GOOD MARKETING TAKES TIME

Frequently design firms start to look for a marketing executive only when they are in serious need of new business. Realize it often takes six months or longer to see some positive results. Are you prepared for this long-term investment? What kind of promotional material do you already have to support this effort and how much have you budgeted for a new collateral piece? Even a very capable salesperson is seriously handicapped without good marketing materials. Helping to develop the new sales brochure should be considered part of the job. Put yourself, figuratively if not literally, in the marketing person's seat. Recognize that there will be downtime during holiday periods when it is hard to schedule new business meetings. Other responsibilities that make good use of these slow times are writing press releases and articles, drafting pitch letters, collaborating on Christmas/New Year's promotional mailings, researching and reading current management and business books and magazines, and updating the database program. It is also an excellent time to review and refine the Marketing Plan direction with the firm's principals.

BUDGETING

The amount a design firm spends on marketing depends on a number of factors: the size of the office, number of years in business and status of existing self-promotion materials. If this is a small, new company, there must be an initial investment in establishing a system that will be used for the next three or four years. So although this outlay will seem considerable at the outset, remember that it will be spread out over a long period of time. A young practice can project a professional, competent image from the start without being extravagant or pretentious. Once you have created your stationery system, you will need some kind of capabilities brochure. This can be anything from a folder or binder comprised of recent laser-printed projects, to a full-color booklet. The key is to create a flexible arrangement that can be added to and tailored to various types of presentations. Generally speaking, the budget for the annual marketing/self-promotion program ranges from 7-15% of gross revenues. Design firms may express these expenses in different ways: per unit cost plus postage, printing and mailing, and so on.

A GOOD FIT

In addition to what a resumé tells you about a candidate's experience, there must be a rapport between you and your marketing person. In a sense, your marketing person is your clone, representing not only your office and work but the spirit and ethic of your company. If yours is a laid-back, casual work environment, with fun clients and playful design, obviously it would be a mistake to hire a conservative, corporate type of account executive, no matter how qualified . . . it's simply not a good fit.

THE SELF-STARTER

Marketing can often be a lonely job, with constant pressure to bring in new clients, one's own performance anxiety and a rather distant relationship with the rest of the staff who don't really understand what an account executive does. Telephone burnout is common in a job that demands 10 to 12 calls an hour, or more that a hundred phone calls a week, with a 1-2% success rate. A good marketing and sales person knows how to maintain his own momentum, and is a self-starter who enjoys the independence of meeting and exceeding his own goals. Pace yourself. The best times to call are mid-morning and mid-afternoon. Best days: Monday afternoons through Thursday.

Nobody can successfully operate in a vacuum. It is important for the head of the firm to know what you are doing on a regular basis. Accountability is vital to the success of the job, and a Weekly Call Report and Update is mandatory. Even if you are doing your own marketing, you should also be keeping these records to track every phone contact and presentation meeting. Two good database software programs for this are Telemagic and Act!.

STAYING MOTIVATED

Keeping yourself motivated is a continual part of the job, and establishing a personal system of goals and rewards is an important way to maintain energy and confidence. Every motivational system or philosophy has something in it that you can use.

Have a few motivational audio tapes to listen to in the car (perhaps on the way to a meeting), while exercising or just taking a walk. The following tapes will introduce you to some new ideas and put you in a positive, enthusiastic frame of mind. This suggested list of audio books represents only a few of the many good ones available.

Beckwith, Harry.
Selling The Invisible.
Time Warner Books, 1997.

Covey, Stephen.
The 7 Habits of Highly Effective People.
Simon & Schuster Audio 1989.

Coates, Bill.
The Road Ahead.
Penguin, 1996.

Hill, Napoleon.
Selling You!
Audio Response Tapes, St. Martins Press, 1988.

LeBoeuf, Michael PhD.
How To Win Customers and Keep Them For Life.
Simon & Schuster Audio, 1987.

Cohen, Herb.
You Can Negotiate Anything.
Audio Renaissance Tapes, 1990.

Peters, Tom.
The Pursuit of WOW!
Random House Audio Books, 1994.

Ries, Al, and Jack Trout.
The 22 Immutable Laws Of Marketing.
Harper Business, 1992

THE BUSINESS COSTUME

At the risk of sounding like a fashion magazine, I agree with many of those self-improvement stories about dressing for the professional world and acquiring a more sophisticated presence. There truly is a male and female "business costume." More strict in some places than others, they help to make a statement about yourself and your company, and is as much a part of the presentation as the portfolio. It makes the selling job easier when you confidently arrive at an important client meeting wearing a suit. You will probably be presenting to a similarly suited executive. This immediately positions you, sartorially speaking, on a peer level. Since you are representing a creative service you can wear wild neckties or exotic colors—whatever expresses a sense of style—as long as you look like a professional. Of course, in cities like Miami and Los Angeles, this rule might be reversed, "casual" being the operative style, so be aware of the corporate culture where you are going. In Montana, I hear, clients show up for meetings in jeans and boots, or ski wear, and often with a four-footed friend.

THE SOUND OF SUCCESS: COLD CALLING

Looking successful can get you in the corporate door, but sounding successful will get you the appointment. Pay attention to your tone of voice as well your speech, especially on the phone. If yours is a low, monotone voice, work on it until you develop an engaging, conversational tone. Speak clearly and briefly, don't use slang, don't ramble or hesitate. You want this call to sound relaxed and friendly, not canned. Practice at home with a tape recorder and try out on a few friends in the office. Do some role-playing. Let them deliver the typical brush-off lines like, "I don't have the time, we are very busy this month;" "We are happy with our present design resource;" and "We don't need anything right now." Ask for their comments and suggestions.

Speak as an equal; assume that you are talking with an intelligent colleague. Be informal but polite. A sales call should be short, qualify the prospect and ideally provide you with a scheduled appointment.

"Hello. This is _____ from _____ Design.

I'm following up on the letter (brochure) I sent you last week."

It is better to send some information about your company before you call or you will hear, "send me something;" and then have to start the calling process all over again.

Does she remember the brochure? Describe, if necessary.

"It's the one in the red, black, and silver envelope" (anything that would make it stand out). Be aware of the fact that that this person has stacks of design capabilities brochures in her office, and receives daily solicitations like yours. Be determined but considerate.

"We have done a series of successful pieces for

_____, _____, _____ (name two or three clients in related industries) *and I think our experience with these companies would make us a good fit with your company."*

By listing companies or industries that are recognized by the prospect as relevant to her needs, she finds your message more credible. If you have won an award for one of these, or if it appeared in a magazine or newspaper story, now is the time to mention it.

If you do not yet have an impressive client list, you should develop some kind of hook to get their attention. For example, *"We have done some very effective two-color brochure design that shows how to save money on your next job without sacrificing impact."*

"I'd like to have the opportunity show these projects to you. When will you have 30 minutes in your schedule for a meeting?"

Tip: Never ask a question that can be answered by "No." "When" is far better here than "can."

At this point all the cues will come from the prospect. If she says they have no present needs, ask for a specific future date when you may recontact her. Keep this date, politely reminding her that she told you to check up at this time.

If she says she is happy with her present designer, ask who they are.

It is especially helpful to know who your competition is, it tells you what level of quality she hires.

Ask whether you should continue to keep her on the mailing list, and if not, can she refer you to someone else in this company, or another she knows, who might be more interested in your services. There is no reason to continue sending material to someone who is not a likely prospect, but if she does not discourage future contact, then the door is still open. Don't push; be friendly yet professional. This is only the first call. When you call again, and most likely you will, she should have some pleasant recollection of you or your company. Remember that you are not trying to sell design on the phone; you are making appointments for presentations of your work.

If you don't get through to the person you want, you should make friends with the secretary or receptionist. *"When would be a good time for me to reach her? What is your name? Thank you, for your help,_____. I'll call back then."* The next time, use the secretary or receptionist's name when you call.

Unfortunately, it's possible you may find yourself talking to a machine or a voice mail system. In this case, be just as warm and cordial. Leave a specific message giving the time, who you are, your company, the purpose of your call and when you will call back. Don't routinely expect them to call you back. It is not likely. Keep a log of calls and return calls as promised.

On a good day, when your mood is upbeat, you can make about 50 or more calls. When it starts to sound to you like you are on "automatic," stop. Do something else for awhile or save more calling for tomorrow. If you are in a bad mood, don't call at all. Unless you are a good actor, your bad mood will be contagious.

If this is your own company, you have automatically assumed the marketing/sales role in addition to being the creative head and entrepreneur. Managing the demands of business inside the office and projecting an upbeat attitude outside requires you to have balance and a certain amount of acting ability. The person who has been hired to create and manage new business is entirely responsible for representing the image of the company to the public, and should express radiant confidence and boundless good cheer. Although there will be days when this seems beyond possibility—like losing a good client, not getting a job that you have been trying to land for months, making some kind of gross computer error—get over it; and move on. I once read this wonderful line; "The difference between an amateur and a professional is that a professional can do it again."

The difference between an amateur and a professional is that a professional can do it again.

THE COLD CALL/BLIND DATE

Intelligence, intuition and flexibility are essential qualities for a marketing/sales person. Think of a prospect call as sort of a blind date. You never know what the situation will be like until you get there, but a lot of clues can be found even as you sit in the reception area. Is there a comfortable place to sit, company literature to read, a phone for you to use? Is the receptionist considerate and friendly or chilly and stressed? The culture of the company is right there in the waiting room. If this is a cold, intimidating environment, beware.

Once inside the prospective client's conference room or office there will be other subtle and not-so-subtle messages. What will the pace of this meeting be? Do you sense that this person is relaxed and friendly, ready to chat a bit before getting down to business, or is this one of those harried, " I can give you fifteen minutes to show me the portfolio, and then I have to get back to work" types? It's not a good idea to present the samples immediately if this is a person who prefers to get to know you first, and an equally bad opening to talk about the traffic and weather to a no-nonsense executive. Your approach should express that you are an intelligent potential colleague who is there to offer help, so before you launch into the pitch, pay attention to the signals. It is important to make some kind of impression as a personality, even if it is just a few minutes. If you are impressed with their great view, their sailboat model or today's beautiful weather, comment on it. Try not to begin an initial meeting by complaining about the terrible rain or traffic; it is a negative way to start a presentation.

PRESENTING THE PORTFOLIO

Be prepared. Before you begin to show your work, take the time to express interest in the prospective company. Having read their annual report or a similar magazine or newspaper profile before this meeting, you should be prepared to ask intelligent questions, listen carefully and lastly, show the portfolio. Don't waste time or rush. It is always difficult to decide how much to put in the portfolio. You want to show your range of experience, but quality is more important than quantity in this case. Bring the work you are most proud of, and tailor the presentation, showing projects most relevant to this company. If this is a bank, leave out the pantihose packaging program. However, if you came up with an especially creative solution for an unrelated business that shows your firm's solid thinking process, include this. Convey your pride in the work and always refer to your design office as "we," not "they."

Organize and orchestrate the presentation to conclude with examples closest to their own needs. Explain what each design problem was and how it was solved. Tell why this project was successful in reaching your client's business objective. If you are showing a video or slides, be sure to also bring samples of the actual printed pieces so that the scale and tactile qualities can be appreciated. Once you have closed the portfolio, take the time to answer questions thoughtfully, and if you don't know an answer, say so, and promise to find out and report back. Don't be abrupt or seem as though you're in a hurry to leave; enjoy this meeting. Should you be asked to give a "ball park" figure on the cost of a job, don't commit yourself to a price or delivery time yet. Wait until you are back at your office and have time to fully analyze the project.

Immediately follow up with a letter of thanks, reminding the prospect what you discussed and when to expect to hear from you again. If he has requested an estimate it should be enclosed or promised to be sent out on a definite date. While all the details of the meeting are fresh in your mind, write a Call Report of what happened as soon as you get back to the office, and enter it in your sales call report database. If this was an especially important presentation, have an internal debriefing session to share this information with staff members so you can all learn where improvements can be made. It is amazing how easy it is to forget what was said or promised in the excitement of the moment. Put it in writing, even if it's just for yourself. Writing reports may seem boring or unnecessary, but believe me, this paperwork can save your life.

Writing reports may seem boring or unnecessary, but believe me, this paperwork can save your life.

3

THE INTERNAL AUDIT:
The Foundation of a Realistic Business Plan

The internal audit is a difficult exercise to do for yourself. Objectivity and self-criticism are rare skills to find in designers who are often sensitive to criticism, but an evaluation of the company has no meaning unless it is absolutely honest. You probably could use some help, so this would be an appropriate time to think about hiring a marketing consultant to conduct a brief, objectively focused analysis of you and your business. The results will provide information about your practice that is both fresh and pragmatic. The research starts with an in-depth discussion about your personal and professional long-range objectives and ends with a formal Business Plan. Occupied with the stresses of the daily management of your office, it may have been years since you took the time to express these dreams and ambitions in writing. Too many people continue to operate in a "Have To" or "Habit" mode. Explore beyond these boundaries. By learning what kind of work gives you the most satisfaction and looking at your portfolio, client and project types, size and profitability, an accurate profile of your firm begins to emerge. As you take the time to evaluate and identify your capabilities, you should also identify what kinds of companies you most enjoy working with.

YOUR DREAM PROJECTS

If you love the glamour and excitement of music and films, you will naturally gravitate toward an entertainment industry-based business. Many opportunities exist for print, film and new media design. A person who brings a genuine interest, knowledge and enthusiasm for the industry is a valued partner.

A highly disciplined, three-dimensional type of designer finds collaborating with architectural firms on identity, environmental and signage programs a rewarding specialization. The ability to work with blueprints, develop way-finding systems and manage complex, long-term projects in addition to solving graphic design problems can lead to a lucrative practice.

If *The Wall Street Journal* is your idea of a good read, then financial services marketing and corporate annual reports are compatible with your interests. Cultivate relationships within this area by joining groups and organizations that attract this kind of membership. For example, the National Investor Relations Institute has local chapters throughout the country. The membership directory is composed of investor relations professionals who are excellent prospective clients.

Some design people have carved out a niche that includes advertising with graphic design. Their advertising/design firms are expert in providing strong copy and market-driven ads as well as well-conceived collateral materials. These individuals enjoy and respect the challenge of creating images that sell. Package design specialists also respond well to research-based, user-focused projects. There are no rules about how or what combinations of talents can be marketed. It is entirely a matter of what you want to do and what your market needs.

Not all design firms are located in places where you would expect to find a range of new client possibilities, but designers who have identified the specialized areas they want to work in do not allow themselves to be limited by location, and have managed to find distant clients who come to them to them for their expertise. Even offices that describe themselves as "generalists" are selective about identifying their projects and clients. Today's modern telecommunications technology allows us to work with clients anywhere in the world, or anywhere in the neighborhood.

Two actively designing partners in the small west Los Angeles office, Cohen Godefroy Associates, wanted to spend more time on their creative work and less time driving to meetings. By researching the number of potential client companies within a five-mile radius, they determined that there was more than enough business in that area. The message that there was a nearby, fun-to-work-with firm providing a range of high-quality design services became the theme for a series of effective, inexpensive mailings. Business increased dramatically the first year. By aggressively targeting their marketing effort to a specific group and continuing to reinforce the message, the partners proved that they did not have to become bigger or travel further to make their business grow.

No two offices are the same. Each design firm is driven by a special mixture of personal values, ambition and talent. The success of a business, any kind of business, is in recognizing and developing this unique combination of factors into a strategy for finding new clients and keeping the best of your existing ones.

No two offices are the same. Each design firm is driven by a special mixture of personal values, ambition and talent.

INTERNAL AUDIT WORKSHEET

Personal and Professional Goals:

In five years I would like my office to be _____

Bigger? Better? How? _____

Would you like the office to stay in it's present location
    or move? _____

What would be the ideal home setting for you? _____

Describe your dream office _____

What would make your professional life more satisfying?

A partner to share the management responsibilities?

Larger staff? New equipment? Better clients?

New business? More income?

What is the profile of your ideal job/client?

Are you best at sales concept, execution or management?

Do you enjoy collaborating and interacting with clients?

Do you prefer working in the office with staff?

What kind of additional support do you need?

How do you relax and recharge?

What are your gripes?

What do you like most about the design profession?

How do you think the profession will change in 5 or 10 years?

Analysis of Competition

Who are your local competitors? (list five to ten firms)

How is their office and work similar to yours?

How does their office and work differ from yours?

Do they charge more? Less? The same?

What can you do to distinguish your firm from this group?

PORTFOLIO REVIEW

Spread out all of the work you have produced in the past two or three years. Put the work you are especially proud of on the left, separate from the projects that simply pay the rent. Study your best work carefully and identify the scope of the project. Was this a single brochure or an ongoing series of collateral materials? Are you still working with this client? If not, why? Was this job profitable?

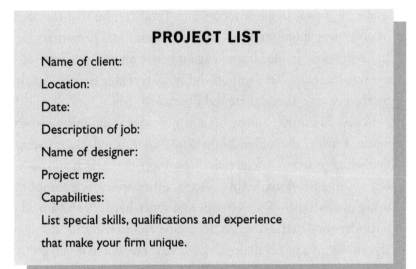

PROJECT LIST

Name of client:

Location:

Date:

Description of job:

Name of designer:

Project mgr.

Capabilities:

List special skills, qualifications and experience

that make your firm unique.

This selected group of projects above represents the strongest core of your business, demonstrating what you do best and for whom. This clear-eyed assessment of your capabilities and experience is the beginning of a workable business plan.

THE TOO MODEST ADMAN

A few years ago I met with the owner of a small New York advertising and design firm. His background in publishing as the creative director of a highly visible fashion magazine, and later as vice president and creative director of an award-winning ad agency, gave him the ability to understand the editorial environment that supports advertising and provided him with extensive experience working with high-level companies. He started his own agency four years ago and attracted a number of the style-conscious, fashion industry clients who were impressed by his outstanding credentials. Although the agency's work was elegant and intelligent, there just wasn't enough new business coming in at a steady rate. The designer, who was an intensely modest young man, hardly typical of the adman stereotype, appeared tense and visibly anxious. Frequently running his fingers through his hair, he spoke hesitantly in a low monotone. I was certain that this lack of poise was apparent at his client meetings and presentations. In his previous publishing and agency environments, where selling was someone else's responsibility, he was able to focus solely on the creative assignment and flourished.

Now his most conspicuous problem was selling his own work. Within the office he had not established a consistent marketing program to aggressively promote the agency, and without an organized marketing system, every sporadic attempt to bring in new business was frantic and short-lived. Professionally he understood marketing was necessary; emotionally, he was paralyzed. From a pure talent perspective there was so much going for this agency. What would it take to make it a strong and viable business? The more we looked at his practice the more obvious it was that he needed a partner to assume the marketing role because he was overwhelmed by the responsibilities of developing new business. It was not easy to convince him that he had to let go of some of the control of his practice in order to survive, but eventually he started looking for a person to share his values and vision. It took more than a year before he met a woman with an excellent background in advertising sales. She had the charm, energy and drive that he lacked, and his offer gave her the chance to be a partner in the kind of agency she had always dreamed of. The chemistry between them was right, and

There was so much going. What would it take to make it a strong and viable business?

with much-needed mutual support, both the partners and the business are now doing well.

When a designer begins his career working for a large organization he takes for granted many things—proposals and letters are written, new business come in, and bills get paid. For his creative efforts he gets a salary and spends little or no time wondering how all of this other activity happens. If the boss is pleased with his work he gets a raise and continues happily at his desk. Years pass, and he may or may not dream of having his own office. Circumstances may drive a designer in to instant entrepreneurship, like being fired or laid off. Sometimes you unexpectedly just get kicked into business. What starts out as a series of temporary freelance jobs, becomes a design firm. Whether you are planning to have your own practice or not, an understanding of what it takes to run a successful business is necessary if you want to contribute more to a job than just renting your head and hands to solve two-dimensional design solutions. The ability to comprehend business strategies and the development of good written and speaking skills makes you a highly valued member of the company.

THE GREEN YOUNG DESIGNER

Recently I consulted with a young designer who bravely opened his own office soon after graduating art school. In business for less than five years, his freelance practice supported him and eventually two assistants, but the work load was determined by whatever he could get, frequently "quick and dirty" assignments. Some projects were low-paying, mundane jobs that he barely managed to resuscitate; others were studio assignments that brought in production work from large, over-worked in-house corporate design departments; few represented the kind of design he hoped for. His clever self-promotion pieces had resulted in new clients, but he lacked the confidence to position his office as a serious design resource rather than a low-cost, quick-turnaround, free-lance emergency room. He also hated to go out and personally sell the work. In addition to being shy, he feared the inevitable rejection, which is probably why he had relied on those phoned-in little jobs for so long. After we completed the survey of his clients, he realized that he had earned the respect and credibility of his best customers, who really wanted to see more of him. Now was the time to move up to the next level. Together we made a plan to raise fees and develop a broader market within the entertainment industry, where he had found an encouraging niche. He recently sent me a sample of a beautiful, elegantly-produced record company catalog that clearly showed that he is reaching his objective.

Even a well-established firm reaches a point in the business when a serious reevaluation is necessary. Sometimes a long-standing client company suddenly changes its strategy or product and you find that you must adopt new skills or knowledge in order to keep the business. You also have to anticipate the fact that old clients may switch to another design office, since surveys tell us that the average client relationship is about five years. One year you are the hot new design firm in town. A few years later, you're not. Don't get too comfortable—it happens.

One year you are the hot new design firm in town. A few years later, you're not.

THE MOST COMMON DESIGN FIRM PROBLEM

According to David Baker, president of ReCourses, in Nashville, Tennessee, a management consultancy for creative and non creative companies, "The most common design firm problem is a lack of consistent marketing. Although referrals are always flattering because they indicate satisfied clients, from a marketing standpoint they only assure more of the same type of business. They result in a reactive activity, not proactive activity. Marketing is the only predictable method of managing a business' future, even out work-flow and expand into desired areas. It is also the surest way of shaping the perception prospective clients will have of your firm."

SMALL IS BEAUTIFUL

"Small is beautiful" could be the motto of this firm, which had grown from a one-person studio to mid-sized one with seven employees, then scaled back to three people. Although it is natural to assume that every successful office will eventually grow bigger, a larger office also requires more clients and projects in order to support the expanded staff. For Petrula Vrontikis, of Vrontikis Design Office in Los Angeles, the studio she thought she wanted became a burden. In the nine years she has been in business she's earned an excellent reputation and won many awards. For her, the bigger, more complex business model did not work. Now with a scaled-down practice, Vrontikis is happily doing terrific work for high profile clients and is more profitable that ever. Her previous experience with an in-house business manager and a formal plan established her good marketing habits, and she remains very committed to consistent self-promotion, ongoing client relationships, and service. This firm has found the quality clients and projects it most wants; now the challenge is to maintain, or even top, this level of achievement. The lesson here is that success and profitability have nothing to do with size. You have to take the time to analyze what kind of office will be most fulfilling personally and professionally.

A designer's creativity has to extend to all aspects of his work, including marketing, and he must continue to stretch and grow in order to compete. Often emerging technologies can create fresh opportunities for the aware, well-informed designer. For example, just a few years ago new media like CD-ROM and Websites did not even exist. We are living in such a fast-paced, ever-changing world that nobody can afford the luxury of being too comfortable or complacent. For the designer who is just entering the profession, there are more choices available than ever, and the design profession is maturing and expanding. Intelligent people who can bring more to the work than the ability to create competent two-dimensional solutions will continue to be in great demand.

Maybe you are a designer who, after years of doing the same kind of projects, is simply bored and now seems like the right time to pursue fresh and different challenges. Before you undertake this new direction you need to know what you want to accomplish, what kind of work is most satisfying to you and what kind of jobs are the most profitable. How can you learn to constructively exploit your previous experience and capabilities?

SPECIALIZATION

How can you learn to constructively exploit your previous experience and capabilities?

For a design firm in a coastal California city, targeting the specialized area of food packaging was a result of the principal realizing that his broader client market was shrinking. He recognized that there was too much competition and less work for the many design generalists in the region, but he liked living and working where he was and did not want to relocate. He realized that his previous experience in food packaging had given him invaluable knowledge about packaging production technology and U.S. Department of Agriculture regulations. He knew he had an edge, and wisely capitalized on this through his marketing communications. Despite not being located in a major urban manufacturing center, his firm has attracted clients for its considerable expertise, and he has won many design awards for outstanding work. By becoming a specialist he took a risk that he would be turning down other kinds of projects, but as the business grew, he saw that he had made a wise decision. He is happy that he was able to stay in a place he loved without compromising on the quality of his business.

GENERALIZATION

Not all designers have the opportunity or desire to specialize, and would find the prospect of doing the same kind of jobs very confining. With a highly motivated marketing person to pursue new business, a design firm can cast a broader net, reaching a wide range of clients. In Des Moines, Iowa, not commonly associated with innovative design, Sayles Graphic Design is a small, "hot" shop with an aggressive marketing strategy. Although John Sayles and partner, Sheree Clark, joke about their "Art" and "Smart" departments, this division of labor allows John to concentrate solely on the creative aspect of the business. Clark's ability as a charming, natural salesperson has generated a great deal of highly favorable publicity about the firm through a series of self-promotion pieces, and her energetic efforts have paid off with bigger and better projects in corporate identity, print collateral, packaging and recently, restaurant interior design, signage and menus. In addition to their successful business partnership, the couple has promoted their personal lifestyle as collectors. "We live and breathe design," they say. "Our studio and home are filled with examples of period design from the 1930s and 40s." Establishing themselves in the local media as design arbiters has certainly translated into increased visibility, which has led to new business opportunities. This marriage, literally, of work and personal life is a credit to the pair's confidence in their special combination of talents.

As all of these case studies show, an internal audit of your firm is not a grim Internal Revenue Service-type of exercise, but a positive step toward making your vision of a fulfilling personal and professional life a reality. The benefit of this self-analysis is a greater awareness of your strengths and weaknesses and the knowledge that you are capable of changing the structure and direction of your practice. Realizing that you are not necessarily locked into the present way of operating is a very liberating dis-

An internal audit is a positive step toward making your vision of a fulfilling personal and professional life a reality.

covery, and gives you a resilience and power that you may not have had before. A successful audit also requires that you be seriously committed to taking whatever future actions are necessary to reach your goals. Understanding your business from within now prepares you to take the next step—seeing yourself from the clients' point of view.

THE BUSINESS PLAN

No matter what business you are in, you need a business plan, a road map, to guide you. The information gathered in the previous exercises should motivate you to create a workable strategy to reach your future objectives. It does not have to be long or complicated, but it is an important document that should be referred to and updated on a yearly basis.

Software packages for business plans are available and are useful as guides. Although most are general and not specifically geared toward design studios, some design business books include business plans that can be downloaded. Shop around to see what is presently being offered. You should consult with your accountant to help you with the financial planning section, Projected Profits.

A number of the elements of this plan—Profile of Principals, Mission Statement and Description of Services—will continue to be used in a number of other applications in the future such as press releases, proposals and your capabilities brochure copy.

Why have I included a business plan in this book on marketing? Basing your future on real data and financial projections puts you in a better position to choose how how your firm will grow, and who will be a profitable client. Information is power, and the more you have the stronger your company will be. The Business Plan is the most important working document of your business. Update every year and refer to it whenever you need to keep yourself on track.

Information is power, and the more you have the stronger your company will be.

THE BUSINESS PLAN

Cover Title Page
Table of Contents

Business Plan / Page One
Summary

This a summary of the total plan, offering an overview of your company, its projected potential, and a report on your present and future financial situation. The summary describes, in brief, the size of your firm, (number of principals and employees), year founded, gross income, type of legal entity, (corporation, subchapter S, etc.), what kind of work you do (graphic design services), and a statement of goals for the coming year.

Business Plan / Page Two
Profile of Principals

The Profile is like a resumé, describing the founding of the firm, the skills, education, awards and previous experience of the partners or principal.

Business Plan / Page Three
Description of Office Facilities and Staff

Location of firm, size of space, description of office and computer equipment (leased, owned?) and projected future equipment needs. Number of staff with job titles and description. Outsourced freelance services contracted may also be listed.

Business Plan / Page Four
Mission Statement
In a short paragraph describe the mission of your practice. This is not the place for high-sounding, vague statements but a concise description of all services your firm provides and your measurable goals. Example: "corporate communications, annual report and financial services design with projected plans to grow to a staff of ten within the next two years. Estimated revenue growth to be in the following year."

Business Plan / Page Five
Description of Services
Describe the range of services your office provides, types of clients, their location and the nature of their business.

Business Plan / Page Six
Financial Goals and Needs
Provide past and projected sales figures, target where you would like the business to be financially in the next one, five, and ten years. Discuss present and possible future opportunities and changes in the design profession. Describe the projected skills, additional staff or space, equipment and estimated costs that are necessary to achieve your future goals.

Business Plan / Page Seven

Market Analysis

Describe the present market for your services and analyze the situation with a view of changes that will influence how you will do business in the future. Discuss your strengths and weaknesses, competition and projected business climate.

Business Plan / Page Eight

Market Strategy

This information will be provided within your Marketing Plan, so do this page after you have completed the Marketing Plan (see Chapter 1 page 12). It will include identifying the market for your services (who and where your potential clients are), what your marketing and promotional plans are, (see Marketing Calendar, Chapter 5, page 69) and the budget for implementing this program.

Business Plan / Page Nine

Financial Plans/Projected Profits

With your accountant or business manager, prepare the following to include: an income statement, cash flow statement, and balance sheet with a three-to five-year projection of earnings. This is the heart of the business plan and the place a bank looks to determine if you are loan-worthy.

4

THE EXTERNAL AUDIT:
A Reality Check

The client looms large as a prize, a nemesis and adversary. The designer/client relationship is loaded with apprehension and insecurity. An external audit provides you with immediate, highly valuable information about client perception, your competition, and potential future markets. And while it is possible to conduct your own formal or informal survey, my research and experience has found that the results are more successful if this audit is done by an independent third party, not by your office. Properly done, this is also an extremely time-consuming process, and a survey of 25 to 30 clients will take a consultant at least a month and over 60 hours to complete.

The external audit first involves preparing an up-to-date client list, including contact and company names, titles, addresses and telephone and fax numbers. It also involves composing a letter to introduce the contact person, conducting the actual survey, compiling the survey questionnaire responses with observations and recommendations, and following up with a letters of thanks to the participants. The party conducting the audit begins the job by sending out the survey by mail or fax and often conducts in-person interviews if possible, or fills out the questionnaire with the client on the phone. An oral survey reveals far more than when the client simply writes in the answers, because the conversation can be directed to additional issues not covered, and it is friendlier and more personal. Most clients are uncomfortable about confronting issues directly with the design firm, and although they won't tell you what you're doing wrong, they are surprisingly candid and open to discussing things confidentially with a neutral party.

DARE TO ASK THE CLIENTS

By asking clients about how you can improve the quality of your service, you are saying how much you care about their opinion and business.

Designers sometimes tell me that they would rather not know what the client thinks—they are that fearful about learning the truth, or that arrogant. The fact is, respondents rarely give any truly visceral, negative reports about a firm, and this within the guaranteed protection of anonymity, since all clients are assured that their names will be left out of the final survey. By asking clients about how you can improve the quality of your service to them, you are saying how much you care about their opinion and business. They are sincerely impressed and appreciative of this effort, and whether this questionnaire comes from a large, established office or a small, young firm, the message conveyed is a very positive one.

Keep in mind that this analysis can give you answers to questions you have previously only guessed about, so make maximum use of this opportunity to make this questionnaire very specific to the particular needs of your office. Ask about your presentation skills if you doubt whether you are coming across as well as your competition. Learn whether your customary slide show is still relevant or whether there is a more up-to-date way of showing the work. Are you selling your company effectively? Are your clients aware of all the services you can provide? Find out if the service your staff provides throughout the job is responsive and intelligent. See what they really think about your pricing and how it compares to other designers that they work with. Never assume that because nobody has complained to you that everything is fine. Discovering your shortcomings will allow you to change and develop new strategies based on this reality check.

The following client survey is a composite of a number of those I have conducted. It is a model that serves to illustrate what is covered in a typical audit. Every firm has its own style and way of operating, but there are certain basic client expectations that must be fulfilled. These questions are designed to provide you with important, useful answers. Your own survey should address your immediate and future needs and provide information that will help you focus on improving every aspect of your business, so don't be shy. Ask.

CLIENT SURVEY

Example: "Great Designers + Associates"

Image

1. How long have you worked with the firm ?
2. What kind of projects do you associate GDA with?
3. What is the image (personality) of the firm?
4. Who are their competitors and how does GDA differ from them?

Presentation

1. How did the presentation affect your choice of GDA?

2. What can GDA do to improve their presentation ?

3. What other firms do a better job and why?

4. Does their capabilities brochure represent them effectively?

Creative Team

1. Was the team sufficiently informed in the project to meet your needs? (Research)

2. Did the firm's principals participate as much as you expected?

3. Do you prefer working directly with a designer or are you equally comfortable with an account manager?

4. How would you describe the completed project in terms of your expectations?

Service

1. Did you have a good working relationship with supporting staff as well as the principals of the firm?

2. Were calls returned promptly and messages taken courteously?

Scheduling

1. Were you sufficiently informed on the progress of the job? Told in advance how your delays would affect the delivery or completion date?

2. Did GDA meet deadlines?

Billing

1. Were bills easy to understand?

2. Can forms be improved?

3. How did the final bills compare to the original estimate? Any surprises?

Proposals / Estimates

1. How big a part does the proposal/estimate play in awarding the project?
2. What is your opinion about GDA's proposal? Too long? Too short? Unclear?
3. Do you receive proposals that you prefer to GDA's and how are they better?
4. Is GDA competitively priced? Are they fair?

Marketing

1. Do you enjoy receiving promotional materials from GDA? Are they interesting, informative, necessary? Why?
2. Have you checked out GDA's Website? Is it useful to you? Do you think this is a good way to market their services?
3. Would you have contacted GDA based solely on their Website presentation? Why?

Capabilities

1. What additional services would you like GDA to provide and why?

Overall Review

1. On a scale of one to ten, what was your level of satisfaction with the project?
   Creativity   Project   Management   Cost
2. What areas can GDA improve in? Problems?
3. If you were to move to another company would you take GDA ? Why?

OBSERVATIONS AND RECOMMENDATIONS

The results of the survey provide the designer with immediate, frank information. Here are some examples of what clients had to say about a varied group of design firms.

Why did you choose "GDA"?

"Their portfolio was impressive, the range of work, personality of the staff and management skills showed quality and integrity." "We were especially impressed by the fact that a small office was willing to also do pro bono work in the community." "The office was large enough to handle the project and had the right 'look.'" "Their own capabilities brochure was good and the initial presentation was excellent."

How would you describe the completed job in terms of your expectations?

"It was a great success in terms of quality and appeal. We were surprised by its simplicity." "If I wasn't pleased, it would not be completed!" "Too many changes. It took too much time." "I'm happy, but their thinking is not at an ad agency level. Words are important."

Scheduling: Were you adequately informed about the progress of the job?

"No! I had to keep calling them up. I don't want to have to pay for rush charges if it's their delay. "The project management was the best I've ever worked with. They pushed the suppliers to the max." "The design outcome is more important to me than schedules." "They need to be more timely in responding, take the initiative, be proactive."

Billing: How did the final bills compare with the original estimates?

"Expensive! High prices for high-quality talent and management. They give a lot of value for certain strategic projects, but they're too costly for the more ordinary jobs." "The follow-up or 'incidental work' is always higher than it needs to be." "Why do they send out invoices on that fancy three-color, two-sided letterhead?" "I go to them with a budget and they meet it competitively. With small companies I end up spending more than I thought I would."

What areas can "GDA" improve in? Where are there problems?

"I see some problems in their pricing. They are very inflexible. They need to consider the customer's point of view." "The partners are hard to negotiate with, intimidating. Our concerns regarding costs got in the way of an otherwise good relationship." "They should learn to show some appreciation. I have recommended them a number of times and they never thanked me or let me know if this resulted in a job." "Attitude. I find them self-defeating and defensive. This is a business situation, not a personal one. How about being more sensitive to my needs?"

CROSS-SELLING

When asked what kind of projects they associated with the design firm, clients invariably cited only the specialty that they had hired them for, and were often unaware of the designer's range of capabilities. It is the designer's responsibility to take every opportunity to cross-sell in their marketing efforts to prevent losing business from an on-board client. The most valued clients understand how you work and know how to integrate your services into their team's program. If you have already proved that you are able to speak their language and understand their concerns, no time will be wasted in explaining, defending and continuously selling yourself. Educating a client can be difficult and frustrating, and from the opposite side, educating a designer can be too!

THE BEST CLIENTS

The assumption that clients know nothing about design is outdated and untrue. Increasingly, clients want to be actively engaged in the creative process, and wise designers welcome them. Often coming from the creative services themselves, sophisticated clients ask practical questions and are not intimidated by the design process. When asked what the most critical element in a working relationship is, they frequently rate project management above creativity or cost. The old picture of an ideal client as a generous, silent, patron-of-the-arts is no longer realistic or desired. There is now more high-quality design in our environment, and proportionately more good designers and clients. To be successful, designers must learn what drives the client's needs and truly grasp business priorities. By discovering how to analyze problems within a business context you will become a true strategic partner. This requires that you go beyond esthetic considerations and learn new skills. It may even mean literally going back to school to get them.

Good clients are made, not born. Here are some wise comments from both sides:

A good client is not born. It takes experience and maturity. I don't want to be looked upon as The Client. I don't want to be "serviced."

From the Clients

"A good client is not born. It takes experience and maturity. I don't want to be looked upon as The Client. I don't want to be serviced." I want to work with a firm that has mutual interests and is willing to share the risks and rewards of the project."

"We have our own corporate design philosophy and look for a good fit. It's not just a matter of the portfolio, it's a talking, communicating relationship. The client must be willing to share a lot of sensitive information."

"I look for talented people who understand the issues and are willing to hook up with an established system. In our company's fast-paced environment, designers must work quickly. I rely on their fresh perspective to help us continue this program and make it simple."

From the Designers

"A good client talks at the beginning and listens at the end. A bad client listens at the beginning and talks at the end. The communication process begins with words."

"A good client situation is a good match. If clients already have a concept, it would be a mismatch to hire a primarily conceptual designer. The best client for our firm is one who is looking for the least pat solution."

"A client can be incredibly demanding and still be a great client. We will knock ourselves out to please him because we know he really cares. We may not always agree, but we share a mutual objective."

GOOD SERVICE IS THE KEY

What I found as a result of talking to clients is that they are much less fickle than designers may think, and are eager to continue and protect a good working relationship. The key to this is excellent account service and project management. Designers who want a larger share in the business world as partners and strategic planners must be vitally concerned about service. And the best way to find out how you are doing in this area is to ask the client. In addition to finding out how you are doing, the survey also tells you what you are really selling. As some of the client comments above illustrate, the designer is selling his objective, creative thinking and intelligent management of the project as much, or more, than design.

Leslie Smolan, partner of Carbone Smolan Associates in New York, says about their survey, "After almost 20 years in business, we felt a need to get an objective view of how we were doing. How did our creative product compare against our competition? Did clients feel they got value for money spent? Were our people, including the firm's principals, delivering the level of service we aimed to provide? This exercise was an extremely useful one. We got immediate resolution of issues we had often wrestled with. For every issue we voiced concern about, we got concrete feedback. Client comments even went so far as to suggest additional services they would like to see us provide. From all perspectives, the survey was a useful management tool that has helped provide tangible benefits, enabling us to improve all areas of client service and look at new opportunities to expand the business."

It is not necessary to be a big, successful company before you ask your clients how you're doing. For a small design firm, the client survey is critical because it tells you where you need to pay more attention and gives specific information on which you will base some future improvements. The following revealing observations and recommendations are from an audit I did for a small environmental design office:

It is not necessary to be a big, successful company before you ask your clients how you're doing.

Personality: Clients describe your personality as "articulate, responsive and approachable," but they also mention an "artistic temperament that does not always take criticism gracefully." Watch this.

Image: "Professional, friendly and attentive" and less positively, "not a businessman, painfully growing, chip on his shoulder."

Capabilities: Many of your clients are not aware of the full range of your services and your brochure is so low-key and discreet that it is hard for the reader to easily find this information. A list of capabilities and clients would accomplish this simply.

Competition: It is impressive that you are compared with larger, more established design firms. Smart clients realize that although small, you have the ability to deliver equal quality at less cost, and although this presents a certain risk on their part, you have a number of clients who are supportive and loyal.

Expectations and the Completed Project: Answers relating to expectations range from absolute delight to total disappointment. There is general agreement that there are problems regarding communications, follow-through and initiative. Your project management is your greatest weakness and must be improved immediately.

Pricing: Pricing is not a problem in fact you may be underpricing in some cases. Clients are willing to pay for quality if excellent service is included.

It was gratifying for me to see how quickly this information was translated into positive action by the designer once he had the answers to his most worrying concerns. The external audit is the single most positive tool you can use to improve your practice. The resulting knowledge allows you to focus on better project management with existing clients, and will lead to more profitable and creatively fulfilling new business.

ON PRESS / THE ANNUAL REPORT CLIENT

The annual report project is a particularly stressful experience, and last-minute changes and alterations, often while at the printer, are inevitable. No matter how harmonious the working relationship may be between the designer and client, when this kind of job enters the production phase, that confidence may be tested. Linda Blount-Strauss, Vice President of Corporate Communications/Investor Relations, Benton Oil and Gas Company, comments, "I think designers and printers need to pay more attention to educating clients about the entire production process, from the start through the final printing. I know my on-press anxiety is a result of things that I don't fully understand. The printer and the designer leave the client in a waiting room full of high-calorie food while they run off and change things. It makes me feel that they don't want the client to understand the process."

The highly technical and complex color printing process certainly cannot be taught in a single visit, but there are certain key points that can be pointed out to the client, "flagged" in advance, as critical to the cost of the job. When a client is shocked by the charges for changes on the final bill, a debriefing meeting between the client, designer and printer should be arranged right away. Nobody wants to lose business or lose face. The client does not want to stop working with a designer she trusts, the designer does not want to lose this client to another firm, and the printer wants to keep this account as well as future business from the designer. Each person should identify where things went wrong and be able to acknowledge their mistakes and responsibilities. Rememember, everything is negotiable, so sit down and work it out. People tend to argue costs with the designer more easily than with the printer. Maybe this is due to the hum of all that expensive machinery; on-press time seems so fixed, while design time appears variable. Without having to resort to the ultimate cave-in line, "the customer is always right," everyone should finally admit that he contributed to the problem in some way, and the bill can probably be reduced. By demonstrating maturity and tact, all parties should be able to leave this meeting with the feeling that something has been gained, not lost. I recommend a handy little book published by International Paper, *The Pocket Pal*, which explains the basics of print production. It might make a thoughtful gift when you start working with a new client.

Developing stronger, happier client experiences by reducing serious misunderstandings is key to a well-run, profitable business.

Growing a successful design firm takes a lot of skill, vision and the ability to constantly fine-tune your management abilities. When you are working for someone else, the management of the company is something you take for granted, if you are even aware of it at all, but when it is your own office, you need an entrepreneurial attitude that gives you drive and commitment. Developing stronger, happier client experiences by reducing serious misunderstandings is key to a well-run, profitable business—any kind of business. For a design firm, it is particularly important to gain respect for good management skills as well as creative thinking.

TARGETING & TRACKING:
How to Find the Best Clients

Finding the best clients requires much more than knowledge about your firm's experience, capabilities and present business. You must now find ways to best use this information to identify your market. No matter how talented you are in a special area of design, there must be a demand for it. Although large, established firms do not consider themselves limited geographically in their search for new business, a small young company has to be realistic about where its work will come from, and that begins with local prospects.

Previously we discussed how to seriously evaluate what your firm does best, revealed sincere desires about the jobs and clients you ideally want, and discovered how your clients see you. Based

What do you look for in a business story and how does this information apply to your search for new clients?

on these facts, you can begin to identify, locate and pursue the targets.

If you are just building your business, like any kind of business in its infancy, you start with existing relationships including friends, relatives and members of your community. As you become more experienced and more credible, you will start to develop a wish list that focuses on nearby corporations, industries or cultural institutions. Reading your daily newspaper's business section and national business magazines keeps you informed about prospects in your area and beyond.

What do you look for in a business story and how does this information apply to your search for new clients? Is this company similar to others you have worked for, in the same or related industry, or is this an area you are eager to break into? Is the company located within a reasonable travel distance? Prospecting out-of-state can be very expensive and unproductive. Does the CEO of the company sound like the kind of person you admire and would easily relate to? Even if you never meet the president of a corporation, his personality and ethic shapes the entire organization. Is this a promising young company or an established old-guard industry? Ask what your firm can offer them and what makes you a good fit with this prospect.

In a recent business magazine I noticed an article about a temporary employment business that was transformed by an original interior design approach. The story described the concept of creating an attractive, retail-like environment to attract higher caliber recruits. The impact of the redesign was substantial, with a 25% recruitment increase after the remodeling. The young founder of the company had finally hired a restaurant designer for the job after rejecting two unsuccessful attempts by more traditional architectural offices.

What does this article tell me that I can use to convert this target into a client? The founder's unconventional approach to the problem demonstrates original thinking, and my instinct tells me that he could be an excellent client, or could possibly lead me to other like-minded companies. If he has not already hired someone to redesign his graphics, he should certainly make that decision next. My approach would be to first send for some of his company's literature to determine how this material can be improved. Then I would write a brief letter to the CEO expressing my interest in the article and the powerful results that good design obviously had on his company. I would continue by explaining how the redesign of all graphic systems including logo identity, advertising, brochures and internal business forms would be compatible with his new direction. I would tell about my company, design philosophy and clients. Samples or photographs of work and possible articles about my office would be included in the package. I would follow this up with a call within two weeks. When you discover a company with this creative approach to business, you have identified a potentially great client, so keep researching mainstream business publications.

Inc. magazine's annual list of the "Hottest New Companies," for example, provides valuable additions to your database and similar lists published in *Forbes* and *Fortune* are very good. *Fast Company* is an excellent young business magazine. You can buy lists from various sources, but I have not always found them to be up-to-date. Also, purchased lists tend to be much more extensive than an average design firm can use, offering thousands of contact companies when you need only 500 or so. To create your own marketing database, you will need the title, fax and phone number of the person you hope to make the presentation to in addition to the company name and address. This usually requires a call to the company for the name of the right contact person, often the Marketing Director, but in a small company this could even be the President. It is a tiresome task, but sending letters and brochures to the wrong individual is an absolute waste of time and postage. These people seem to change positions frequently or leave for new ones, so plan on updating the list once a year.

THE DATABASE

The goal in building your database is not to create a giant mailing list of thousands of names and companies, but to select a specific group of targeted prospects that will yield meaningful business opportunities. This could begin with 500 names and, by a process of elimination, be pared down to a more likely list of 100 solid potential clients. There is no exact formula number; it depends on where your business is located and how large your office is. In addition, I also suggest that you select a "hit list" of ten companies you would most like to work with, and devote a special effort to landing them. This list can include clients that you previously worked with, contacted prospects who may not have hired you, and companies you admire. Update this list every month, and give yourself a realistic schedule of time within which you will contact them.

TRACKING

Establishing a system of tracking prospects is the foundation of your marketing program. Since it often takes five to ten contacts and many months before you can begin to build a relationship, a good marketing software program, like Telemagic or Act! is extremely useful. With a contact management system you can keep track of mailings, calls and meetings, schedule follow-up action, and keep notes of relevant information like a company's fiscal year-end date, present designer, even the name of the prospect's dog or favorite restaurant. Being organized saves time and keeps things moving.

I once worked for a design firm that was a subsidiary of a large international advertising agency. Their marketing director shared with us a practical theory he referred to as "The Canal Principle," illustrated by a colorful diagram of canals and barges, (the agency being the "barge"). The agency's objective was to create a constant flow of marketing activity to keep the agency moving forward.

At the time, rather early in the development of the design profession's marketing efforts, this seemed to me like a very sophisticated procedure, but now it looks quite logical and straightforward. The process begins by getting answers to the following questions:

PROSPECT QUESTIONNAIRE

1. How do we select our prospects?

Qualify the prospect. Not all companies are a good match for you. You may even want to do a credit check before starting a big job. Establish your own criteria for prospective clients.

2. How much research will we do on them?

At the very least you must read their annual report or some company literature. By the time you present to them you should be familiar with some of the company's history, main players and products.

3. How do we track our contacting?

A systematic record of all mailings and calls is kept in the database. Quarterly contact is average. It is not unusual for it to take years before a company will be ready to change designers. Be persistent.

4. Who do we make the initial approach to and how?

In a large corporation there are potential prospects in a number of areas: investor relations, communications, marketing, and public relations. Calling these departments will give you the prospects' names and titles. After the initial contact, you will know where your best opportunities are and you can continue to develop the connection from there.

5. How do we follow up and how often?

Certainly you will follow up immediately after the presentation, but if the presentation is more of an introduction to your work than a pitch for a specific project, you will want to keep in touch every three or four months.

6. What will the presentation be and who will make it?

If this is a big project for a large company, you, the principal of your firm and at least one other person will attend the meeting. This may be your assistant, a senior designer, or the account executive. The presentation can be as simple as showing samples of your work and telling the "problem/solution" story or a multimedia extravaganza created for this particular meeting. It depends on the scope of the job. Tape the meeting or have someone take good notes.

7. What is our action response to a request for a pitch?

This is "ad-speak." An ad agency will spend a lot more time and money on a pitch than most design firms because the final payoff is financially greater. For a design firm, a "request for a pitch" means you do your research, prepare your portfolio and see them as soon as you can.

8. How do we follow up on a failed presentation?

It is important to learn from mistakes. If the presentation failed to get you the project, you should ask the prospect why, as painful as that may be. You should also conduct your own debriefing session in the office.

9. How do we maintain contact with a successful pitch?

Unless the presentation results in an immediate "you're hired!" response, you will want to maintain that positive impression of your firm. Stay in touch by phone or letter. Send them samples of your latest work. Don't be annoying, but stay in the picture.

10. Does this all work?

Yes, it does work. It works because like the barge and canal example, there is a steady flow of activity: targeting, contacting, presenting and performance evaluation. Even the smallest design firm can employ these principles successfully.

WHAT ELSE CAN DESIGNERS LEARN FROM THE AD BUSINESS?

Although an advertising agency is different from a graphic design practice in a number of ways, designers can learn important lessons there. An ad agency is hired, for example, to create an ongoing print media advertising campaign for a year, rather than the project-to-project approach of most design offices. A lucrative, highly competitive business, advertising has even created a rating system to measure the success of its work. Much time and effort is spent researching prospects, clients and competition. Considerable creative energy is invested in good copy and original concepts. Client relationships are vital, and intelligent, personable account executives are highly valued.

Designers, being primarily visual in their orientation, may jump into a new project without enough research on the client company. Eager to try out some new design or printing technique or the latest paper, they do not always pay attention to the real, end-user problems. Copy is rarely given sufficient regard, and is often treated rather like a meaningless texture: in fact, some designers seem to have absolute contempt for copy. Although many hours are lavished on the client during the job, after the work is delivered, months can go by without them ever hearing from you again.

Designers should apply some of the strategies and practices of the advertising business to help to build a smarter, more broad-based firm. Keep your eyes open, do your homework, and be ready and willing to learn from some of the experts.

THE SEARCH AND RESEARCH

Eventually, like a successful hunter, you will develop an instinctive sense of where to find the best prospects.

The search for promising new business requires a considerable amount of patience and preparation. Research includes reading a company's annual report to learning about their product or industry, gathering basic financial information about their past year, and making a record of companies or people mentioned in the press that indicate a change in management or technology, news of company mergers and acquisitions, plans for commercial, entertainment or cultural venus, and any other strategic information that may be the source of new business relationships. Eventually, like a successful hunter, you will develop an instinctive sense of where to find the best prospects. At the same time, you will also be learning about your competition as you question a potential client about whom they are presently working with, ask if and why they are happy with this design firm, and view the previous work they have produced. By paying attention to prospects as they discuss their needs and priorities you will discover additional services to provide and distinguish yourself from the competition.

HITTING THE TARGET

Identifying new business can sometimes be as simple as looking at the downtown skyline and pointing. It once happened to me as I was driving to a shoot in downtown Los Angeles with an annual report photographer. He asked me what kind of clients I was looking for. As the marketing executive for a design firm specializing in annuals, I felt that we needed more immediately recognizable clients to reinforce our credibility. "There," I said pointing to the tallest new skyscraper, "I want that company in our portfolio!" Eventually I was able to make a presentation to the corporation housed in that tower, but I was not optimistic about our chances. In my notes after that first meeting I wrote, "Nice guys, no chance." For the past two years the present design firm had won awards for their annual report's design. Why would this client not stay with them? But, tenaciously, I continued to stay in touch with the nice guys I had met, and was very surprised when they asked us to submit a proposal for next year's book. We got the job, and kept this client for a number of years.

Why, you may be eager to know, did they change designers? Although their latest annual had won prestigious awards from the design community, what it said about the company visually did not convey the CEO's most important message. The handsome, gritty cover shot of oil rig workers did not acknowledge the new retail divisions the corporation had recently acquired. Because shareholders and analysts were questioning the judgment of this move, the cover of the report appeared to ignore this sensitive issue. The chairman had obviously missed this point in the early cover design reviews, and dealt with the problem by changing to a fresh creative team. The object lesson here is not only that "persistence pays," but also "winning prizes does not guarantee client loyalty."

ON THE PROSPECT'S TURF

To target new prospects means meeting them on their own turf. If your area of expertise is in food packaging, then attending national and regional trade exhibitions like the annual Fancy Food Show will give you a chance to see the latest products, packaging and technology as well as to meet key marketing and sales people. Since environmental and signage designers frequently collaborate with architectural firms and developers, you should seek out conferences, seminars and exhibits that inform you about new projects, products and fabrication techniques, plus offer the opportunity to meet personally with the major players in that industry. Annual report and corporate communications designers can learn the language and concerns of their prospective clients by joining professional organizations like the NIRI (National Investor Relations Institute) or the IABC (International Association of Business Communicators). In addition to making new contacts at the meetings, every organization publishes a membership directory that provides additions to your database. By being one of a few design firm representatives there, sometimes the only one, you have a distinct advantage. Make good use of it. Introduce yourself, exchange cards, arrange for a lunch date, but never try to sell your services on the spot; it's not good form, and is too aggressive. You want to be perceived as a professional with a valued expertise, not a peddler.

You continually have to reach out for business by personally being "in the field".

If you have not established a specialized niche for your services, exploring the field in this way can expose you to some good possibilities and expand your network. You continually have to reach out for business by personally being "in the field." New business development involves more than mailing brochures and telemarketing. Occasionally you will be asked to speak or act as a design competition judge for organizations. These engagements are great opportunities to promote your business and position youself as an expert in the field worthy of an investment of time and energy. Feel free to volunteer in these capacities—even if you haven't been approached directly, all organizations welcome this kind of participation.

THE MARKETING CALENDAR

JANUARY New Year's greeting card	**FEBRUARY** Press release	**MARCH** New client/Job announcement	**APRIL** Capabilities brochure
MAY Newsletter	**JUNE** What's new at ___Design	**JULY** Vacation announcement	**AUGUST** Press release
SEPTEMBER New client/Job announcement	**OCTOBER** Sample/Slide Recent job	**NOVEMBER** Press release	**DECEMBER** Hoiliday gift or greeting card

A marketing program needs a schedule, however informal, to assure that you are getting your firm's name out there on a regular basis. One mailing piece a year, no matter how fabulous, does not make a total marketing program. Keep in mind that many other design firms are also sending out material, each one thinking theirs is the most outstanding. Picture these brochures, mail-ers, postcards, T-shirts videos, and CD-ROMs accumulating into large piles on the desks, files, and floors of the intended prospect. How will your message stand out? I was surprised to hear from potential clients that they often get a terrific brochure, save it expecting to be contacted, and never hear from the design firm again. You will get new clients from these promotional efforts, but do not passively wait for them to call you; follow up with a phone call to everyone you mail to. It is good business, good selling, and the best way to begin to build a relationship. The sample calendar offers an example of a monthly marketing program. I do not suggest that you do everything every month, but the minimum is at least four mailings a year, or one per quarter.

TRACKING: CASE STUDIES

Assuming that you have now established a regular marketing program for your office and are diligently sending out memorable, informative or fun promotional pieces, how do you find out if they are bringing you any business? Do you care? For most designers, promotion may be the only "marketing" they do and they definitely expect this effort to pay off. But some people have a different attitude, and consider this more of an exercise in self-expression and good will. 1185 Design in Palo Alto, California with a staff of 30 people and has been in business for 12 years. They have a flexible promotion schedule that switches from year to year—one year a single piece, the next year monthly or quarterly mailings. President Peggy Burke reports that they have no actual tracking method other than direct compliments from recipients. She estimates that they do gain two or three new clients a year this way, but that is not the primary motivation. "Self-promotion is an opportunity for us to showcase the wealth of creativity that our firm offers. We are our own client on these projects, so we can work without any restraints or 'designing-by-committee.' Our portfolio work reflects our efforts combined with

For most designers, promotion may be the only "marketing" they do and they definitely expect this effort to pay off.

the client's taste, but the promotion pieces are a purer example of the firm's potential."

UP Design, a young, small studio in Montclair, New Jersey, has been very enthusiastic about playful self-promotional mailings from the start. Designers Wendy Peters and partner, Gary Underhill have become more organized and focused about promotion in the past few years. "We always do a mailing to announce our vacation closing time, at Christmas and the Fourth of July. In between these times we try to send out press releases or our little UP DATE newsletter every four to six weeks, and send out one or two marketing packages every week to specifically targeted prospects. To track results we use a database system to enter notes and responses and we also enclose a reply card with every mailing. As a result of this program we get two new clients a year, and just about every mailing initiates additional work from an existing client."

Principal Bill Ferguson, at INC Design in Manhattan, is responsible for planning all the marketing of his annual report and corporate communications firm, and he insists that the marketing group track the results of all promotional mailings with follow-up telemarketing calls. Ferguson considers this as an excellent opportunity to engage the prospect in a discussion about their response to the brochure and to learn about their particular needs. "Out of a mailing list of 700 prospects, we gain an average of seven new annual report clients a year, but because new client acquisitions are tied to a marketing program in addition to our mailings, it's difficult to say which clients come to us purely as a result of our promotional efforts. If we never had a relationship with a prospect, and he never heard of our company before, the mailings serve as one of the most effective ways we can introduce ourselves. This keeps us linked to the outside world, and successfully keeps our company name in front of our clients, former clients, prospects and media contacts." By tirelessly promoting the firm, INC creates an awareness of its people, process and quality product. For their kind of clientele, building and maintaining an outstanding reputation is one of the key objectives and they have a good marketing system in operation to assure continuing growth.

One of the primary reasons tracking is so essential is that it transforms the initial cold call or direct mail contact to the start of a working relationship. Rather than constantly coming up with a fresh list of new prospects, tracking allows you to take the contact to the next level.

A confident, large design office in Boulder, Colorado, Communication Arts, Inc., tracks the results of presentations that succeeded or failed based on client interviews. I think this shows real courage. They conduct formal team debriefing meetings in the office, which gives everyone a chance to learn. Partner Janet Martin tells me, " Sometimes the prospect wants to hire an out-of-town (or local) firm, sometimes it's price or maybe personality. When I make a follow-up call it gives me the opportunity to connect even if only to say, "Perhaps we can work with you in the future.' If it is a matter of cost, a client or prospective client may even coach you through the pricing process so your estimate conforms to their budget. One large client company who did not give us the job took me through their decision process in our debriefing meeting and offered to show me the nine other proposals that were considered. After all, we understand that we won't get every job we go after, but it's important to find out why so we can improve the next time."

We understand that we won't get every job we go after, but it's important to find out why so we can improve the next time.

Janet Martin

Clients and prospective clients appreciate that a designer is concerned with service and quality, not only aesthetic considerations. This additional attention shows that you care about them, and this is what service is really about. Targeting and tracking new clients doesn't mean much unless you are equally committed to making the effort to keep them. Even after the job is over, your marketing work should continue. Always anticipate the next project.

CHAPTER

POSITIONING & IMAGE

WHO AM I?

As a designer, one of the hardest things you must do is develop an objective view of your business and create a strategy for positioning yourself in the marketplace. This requires the honest, clear-headed ability to articulate your business goals. You must decide not only what kind of work your firm does best, but identify a future plan that best fits your personal lifestyle. Whether you have decided to be a "generalist" or a "specialist," what makes you and your company unique? How can you improve your capabilities to compete more effectively? Where do you want to take your business?

Your goals will first be expressed in what is referred to as a Mission or Positioning Statement, which appears in your Business Plan (see Chapter 3), and will also be used in a number of formal "boilerplate" applications: proposals, press releases, introductory letters and capabilities brochures. This statement is a necessary part of your company's verbal communication. Too often designers regard this kind of copy as "sort of a gray texture," but prospective clients will actually read it and judge you by what you say, so get it right.

Before we describe your overall objectives, here is a challenge from Hoboken, New Jersey-based promotion specialist Ilise Benum. In her quarterly publication, *The Art of Self-Promotion*, she offers the following useful oral and written exercise called "Your Seven-Word Blurb Worksheet"

Sometimes you have no more than 20 seconds to engage a potential client's interest...on the other hand you may have five minutes to address a group about what your firm does. For a variety of environments, you need to be able to speak about yourself and the work you do. (Hint: Each answer should begin the same way, with more elaboration and details when more words are called for.)

What do you do? (25 words or less)

What do you do? (15 words or less)

What do you do? (7 words or less)!

This seemingly simple assignment is difficult because it forces you to communicate succinctly with non-designers. Unfortunately, the public at large still is not too clear about what "graphic design" is. Describing what you do in seven words or less may appear very elementary, but "civilians" know surprisingly little about the range of the design profession's capabilities. Assume nothing. Explain.

THE MISSION STATEMENT: IN YOUR OWN VOICE

Your mission/positioning statement should be brief, (200 words or less), sincere and in your own voice. If you and your office are casual and informal, this style is part of your image and "corporate voice." If you are more comfortable with businesslike language, use it consistently. Recently I read a mission statement for a very conservative, industrial design company that has been in business for 30 years. The copy sounded crisp and contemporary in an odd contrast to the rather dated style of the work shown. The writing, I realized, was done by their young marketing director and reflected her own upbeat style, not the firm's. What's wrong with that? It sets up an expectation that the principals of the company will be young and cool, and in this case they're not. Remember, the best client relationships are about a good fit. If the prospect can identify with your message and then is disappointed when he meets you in person, you have failed in making a match by creating the wrong image. Be yourself. If someone else is writing the statement, be sure it sounds like you, only better.

YOUR BUSINESS PHILOSOPHY: AN INVITATION

The mission statement tells who you are and what you most care about; it's your business philosophy and should engage the reader in a way that makes him want to meet you. A list of clients and projects may give you immediate credibility, but this does not speak directly to your primary audience, the prospective client. The statement is literally an introduction, a slightly more formal speech than what you might make at a first presentation meeting. It should convey, above all, a desire to participate in a mutually creative process, to collaborate rather than dominate.

THE DESIGN LANGUAGE

Some years ago, Steven Heller wrote a very funny piece in *Print* magazine entitled, "Design Patois: How Do I Love Me?" in which he quoted from anonymous design firm's promotional brochures. "Most designers learn—Lord knows where—that to gain respect in the outside world it is imperative to use officious-sounding language they'd never use in correspondence or conversation. No school exists to teach this stuff, yet take virtually any promotional brochure for a design firm and you will find variations on the following: 'We constantly strive to push the creative edge—to challenge ourselves and our clients to achieve works of distinction.' 'Design is a tool for achieving specific results. Being responsive, we begin each project by learning exactly what results our client expects.' 'Establishing an appropriate, positive emphasis is the key. This, in conjunction with good graphic design, is our special skill.'

These samples of vacuous messages illustrate the point that designers should pay more attention to what they say in print. Yet, according to Heller, most designers represented by statements like these, are in person, articulate, literate individuals. He suggests that they should think twice before hiring someone else to write their copy.

EFFECTIVE MESSAGES FROM DESIGNERS

Within the span of my own career I have seen design studios, little more than sweatshops run by cigar-chomping bosses, become transformed into "firms" presided over by "presidents" in three-piece suits. While the packaging of design services has improved greatly, the ability to express an intelligent verbal message about the value and function of design has not been so successful. A certain defensiveness and insecurity lingers. In general, designers have had to improvise and imitate the business language of their audience, and it often sounds ill-fitting and pretentious. For me, the best copy is brief, sincere and to-the-point.

VOICES: REAL PEOPLE

For example, Vaughn Wedeen Creative, a design partnership in Albuquerque, New Mexico, has attracted a broad range of clients and projects including corporate annual reports, cultural and non-profit promotional literature, retail and hotel identity systems and gourmet food packaging. Rather than subduing their naturally enthusiastic, upbeat voice into "bizspeak," the tone of their brochure sounds believable, expressing who they really are: "Creating original ways to address unique situations on behalf of a wide variety of clientele is a constant way of life for our company. We love to push the possibilities, not succumb to limitations. Change is occurring at an unprecedented pace, and companies are rethinking their means of influencing their audiences. New rules are being written in order to succeed. Creativity is key to prosperity."

This design firm sounds fresh. Their work looks like the message—contemporary, clever, capable. If I were a prospective client, I would definitely want to meet these people. I later learned that the brochure took years to produce because the writer they hired had trouble in achieving the right voice. Finally, in exasperation, one of the partners sat down and wrote it, and this is why the statement sounds so genuine.

In New York City, an established design office with a distinguished client list expresses itself with confidence and poise. " . . . Since we began working together, our emphasis has been on innovative design that is intelligent, memorable and distinctive. Our approach is driven by strong concepts because we know that great design comes from great ideas. Together we have the same goal: insight-producing, exceptional work for clients who want the best." The engaging photograph of the partners in

This design firm sounds fresh. If I were a prospective client, I would definitely want to meet these people.

77

their office reinforces this statement by showing the faces of these two individuals in their professional habitat.

Many capabilities brochures simply show examples of design projects, but I think that adding a picture of the key players leaves a more lasting impression. I have even seen a marketing brochure where the partners themselves, shown in full-page, color photographs, were the message and no work was shown at all. The situation that inspired this unusual concept was that the three partners had recently left a firm, where they had worked together, to start their own business. When they opened the office they had not yet produced any work, but needed a promotional piece to send to prospective clients. The brochure was built around the capabilities of the partners and what they contribute to the partnership: intelligent client communication, design excellence and superior account management. "Behind each award-winning design is a team of people with an extraordinary ability to solve problems and achieve dramatic results, the brochure begins." Then, each partner makes a personal statement:

"We're in a business driven by ideas—and giving these ideas a bold, distinct creative energy is what I think X Design is all about. There's nothing more rewarding at the end of a project than to have a client say that our performance exceeded their expectation."

"For me, the bottom line is a design that's exciting and relevant . . . a design that makes a difference. I spend considerable time researching a project to familiarize myself with my client's company, competition and industry."

"My strength lies in understanding my client's needs and relieving them of many of the daily burdens and headaches, offering practical solutions; in short, streamlining and simplifying an otherwise complex process."

The brochure is remarkable because the words and images are fresh, honest, and inspire client confidence. Remember, the primary objective in sending your brochure is to have an opportunity to meet with the prospective client, or to leave behind a memorable representation of your company. If the work shown, or in this case the individuals introduced, are credible and interesting this will be relatively easy. But this should not be considered a mail order catalog. In a few years, when it was time for the next brochure, the partners described above had some great new projects to show and client stories to tell.

This colorful West Coast designer must certainly have written the following copy. The salty tone is certainly his own voice:

"If you've spent any time at all searching for a design firm, I have no doubt that by now you are immersed in the buzzwords of my business. Now I could treat you to another definition of Design Communications, or tell you about how closely our firms will work together, or how deeply we will become immersed in your business, but the truth is, any design firm will tell you these things. For me the greater truth is this: when you see a good design you can feel it in your gut. Our work speaks for itself. If it speaks to you, please call."

Brash, opinionated words but very true to the strong personality of this talented designer. The challenging message is loud and clear for a prospective client who can stand up to this kind of ego.

Although you are understandably eager to show a handsomely designed brochure with pictures of successful projects, anticipate that your message will also be carefully read. Write your mission statement or business philosophy as though your business depends on it.

Write your mission statement or business philosophy as though your business depends on it.

POSITIONING

As a designer evolves, graduating from a small and hungry practice to a more focused and selective business, a number of tough decisions have to be made. Where you are located certainly affects some of these. The grass is always greener. If you are in a small city it is difficult to grow because there are not many prospective local clients and if you are in Manhattan there are plenty of them, but also an abundance of other designers. How does a creative business distinguish itself from the pack and find success?

Imagine walking into a room filled with 300 prospects. How can you talk to them all? Will you be able to personally hand out 300 business cards? No. As I explained in the last chapter with regard to targeting your prospective business, establishing a position for your practice is equally crucial. In fact, you would not want to work with everyone in that room, and they will not all be attracted to you. Taking a clear, confident position about what you do and who you want to be hired by is the foundation you will build your future on. Like everything worthwhile in life, it involves risk.

AMBITION AND REALITY

Surviving the first few years when any kind of job was welcome, a designer eventually wants to choose the clients and projects that will be more rewarding, personally and financially. This means that you will occasionally have to turn down work and risk losing clients when you raise your fees. One of my clients is now in this exact position and we discussed the problem at a recent meeting. "I want to shoot for the big jobs," he said. "I know I am capable of doing them as well or better than my competitors. I'm talking about the six-figure projects, not the five-figure ones that we are able to easily handle. But prospective clients don't want to hire small offices like mine because they think they won't get the service that big firms offer." Although his ambitious spirit and eagerness are commendable, I can clearly see that his staff and office facilities are minimal and project management and service are problematic, maybe more than he realizes. Positioning and establishing a new set of goals should be based on reality. Shooting for the bigger jobs that are for the present over your head is a mistake. It is better not to take on a big job, than to fail at providing good service and ruin any future prospects with that client.

How can this designer achieve his objectives? In order to grow into the kind of practice he wants, he has to provide himself with the solid support of an adequately staffed, well-equipped office and create a management system that will not fail him or his clients. This will take time and patience, but if he stays focused, he can fulfill his dream. There are no short cuts. Remember, don't promise what you can't deliver.

IMAGE

Someone lent me a book recently written by a couple of bold young advertising agency partners who counseled that to be successful in your business you should lavishly redecorate the office, lease a Mercedes and buy yourself an Armani suit. The premise of the book is that if you look like a winner you will be. Their company, I must add, is in Canada and perhaps being in a different environment, this strategy worked. Then again, maybe advertising agencies are more likely to think this way, but I have a few words of caution. How you impress a new client in order to get that first assignment is one thing; how you keep him is quite another. The true test is serving the client and delivering the job as promised. If you cannot do that, then what you drive or wear makes no difference.

Design is obviously a very visual, style-conscious business, and appearance counts although there is a certain amount of latitude about it. Part of your goal in expressing your mission, your professional goal, is to write a statement that you can live with and really believe. This sincerity makes the work you show even more credible. Some young designers often try to project an image of "the firm" even if they are alone or operating a studio with a partner or an assistant. They write a company profile as if they were an established, old-guard office using a formal corporate language to describe their services, thinking this will impress a prospective client.

There are no short cuts. Remember, don't promise what you can't deliver.

First, give the prospect some credit for figuring out that you have probably only been out of school less than five years and are unlikely to be too solid. Second, recognize that there is an advantage in being a talented, eager design professional. You bring a freshness and enthusiasm to the work, and all things being equal—quality, service, price—there is no reason why you will not be awarded the job just as you are. Third, pretending is not the same as confidence, which can only be earned through successful experience.

Let's assume that you head a small design firm with a few good clients and some awards on the wall. You want more quality work from the best companies in your region. You are an ambitious, creative designer, and a capable manager with a winning smile and a strong handshake. How do you make your office, and yourself, stand out above the competition? What can you say to convince prospects to want to meet, and ultimately, hire you? Before you consider writing anything, begin by reading other design firms' brochures. Get these any way you can, perhaps borrowing a few from a client or vendor. Remember, what sounds great in somebody else's pitch may not fit who you are or what you do. By gaining an appreciation for copy that is well-written as opposed to reheated platitudes, you can decide whether you have the ability to create your own message. If this seems too overwhelming, then definitely hire a professional with expertise in this specialized kind of copy, a writer who understands the graphic design business.

What can you say to convince prospects to want to meet, and ultimately, hire you?

It is hard to focus on your own practice objectively, but during some quiet hours in your office, put in writing why design has meaning in your life, what you hope to achieve with each project, and what is special about how and what you produce for your clients. Express this sincerely, without being either arrogant or condescending. What the message should boil down to is simply, "This is who we are, what we value and why you should consider working with us."

FULFILLING THE PROMISE

This Mission or Positioning Statement will not, in itself, be the source of new business and lasting happiness, but you will benefit by having defined your objectives and image to yourself as well as the world at large. When the business grows you may want to reexamine what you have written and make some changes. No statement should be so permanently established that it cannot be improved and it will probably need to be updated every five years. I have often observed that once this necessary exercise has been accomplished, a designer becomes more confident about his direction and makes business decisions more easily . . . fulfilling his own promise.

OTHER WRITTEN MESSAGES

Your business correspondence—every letter, fax, and E-mail message—represents your office. Do not treat this casually. No spelling errors, typos or incorrect titles should escape your notice. Letters should be brief, to the point and clear. Before you put anything in writing, ask yourself what you really need to say. Don't use old-fashioned, formal business language. Be yourself. Create a series of form letters: Thank You For Your Inquiry, Cover Letter, Thanks For Meeting, etc., and use them. This is a good way to save time and respond quickly with minimal effort.

Press or news releases are a low-cost, effective form of publicity and promotion. Your standard Press Release Form enables you to send out news of new clients, awards, or pro bono projects. These are sent out to local and trade media and may be published there. The press release is a particular form of copywriting, always in the third person, factual, double-spaced, and very crisp in style.

SAMPLE PRESS RELEASE

RELEASE: IMMEDIATE

**Contact: Your Name, Telephone and Fax Numbers,
and e-mail address**

Boston, May 1, 1999

XXX COMPUTER SYSTEMS PICKS ____ DESIGN ASSOCIATES

_____Design Associates today announced that they have been selected by XXX Computer Systems Inc., Cambridge, Massachusetts, to design the XXX 2000 Annual Report. The report will focus on the breadth of the changes at the company during the year, initiated by the return of XXX's founder and CEO, Sandra XXX.

Ms. XXX, 43, founded the company in 1982 with $2,000 in savings and built it into a $200 million supplier of information systems to manufacturing companies. In 1995 she resigned from the day-to-day management of the company. She returned to her full-time roles as Chairman, CEO and President in April of this year.

"The next decade will be the beginning of a whole new range of software to operate with the latest computer technologies," states XXX. "I returned to the company because it is in an ideal position to capitalize on these trends. I view XXX as a $200 million start-up, and have put in place new management and strategies to enable us to build the products to grow the company to a billion dollars." The challenge for ____ Design Associates is to design an annual report that will communicate the energy and entrepreneurial spirit of the company and management.

As one of the East Coast's outstanding design and marketing communications firms, _____ Design Associates has created award-winning annual reports for some of America's most prominent corporations for over 15 years. The XXX Computer Systems 2000 Annual Report is a perfect partnership between a spirited, intelligent company and a design team with unlimited creative and strategic abilities.

In addition to sending the news release to the media, I have also found that sending special press releases to clients, prospects and vendors is an efficient method for broadcasting good news. Releases can be mailed alone or as an enclosure in a letter. This can often be as effective as when the release was originally published.

The process of researching this book has put me in contact with design firms that really "get it." One such firm, The DePuis Group, in Woodland Hills, California, has positioned itself in a number of distinctive ways. For an office with a staff of 30 that has only been in business for three years, marketing and promotion has obviously made a dramatic contribution to its success. The DePuis Group considers itself a market research resource and has created a Web site as a place to teach about the design process by offering a library of forms that can be down-loaded including: marketing briefs, branding and packaging briefing forms.

Steven DePuis says, "Marketing and self-promotion are the most difficult tasks for us. We are our worst clients. Not only is it hard to put aside billable hours for designing and writing, but the process of focusing on ourselves and how we relate to the market is a constant challenge.

"We market in four integrated phases:

1. One-on-one marketing through referrals and contacts
2. Direct marketing to clients, vendors and prospects via bi-monthly mailings of postcards showing an exemplary design solution and the market results
3. Advertising in *The Wall Street Journal* to reach CEOs and other decision-makers within a targeted region
4. Promotional events that showcase the expertise of our people (illustration and 3-D rendering, for example) or our video-conferencing capabilities.

"Marketing and promotion expenditures average between 2-5% of revenues, depending on our current growth objectives. Our strength is a result of promoting a position that has been received as not only different from other design firms, but more relevant to our clients' needs."

By integrating market research into the design process, this firm has gone deeper than most of their competitors and learned to communicate in a language that their clients understand.

Discovering your niche, your edge, is what makes you stand out in the crowd. This is the essence of Positioning.

THE MARKETING & SELF-PROMOTION PROGRAM

Once you have expressed your positioning objectives and values, and determined how you would like your firm to be perceived, the time comes when this information must be turned into action. After considerable research and analysis, examining your company, surveying your clients and targeting the market, the development of an intelligent, realistic marketing program is the logical next step. Think of it as a road map, taking your practice where you want to go, but flexible enough to allow for unexpected changes in the itinerary. A marketing program for a design firm is not the same as the rigid plan employed by a large manufacturing company, and you don't need an M.B.A. to develop one, but it requires discipline, patience and conviction.

The Marketing Program Calendar in Chapter 5 suggests a number of promotional concepts used throughout the year. For a small design studio, this may be considered your entire promotion program: a minimum of four mailings, or one every quarter. In any case, you will need to keep a record to follow up on responses to the mailings, including the number of appointments and new clients, because this information allows you to track and keep score. It is very rewarding to look back over a year and see the results of your self-promotion efforts. The calendar and your database tracking system are key elements in a successful marketing and self-promotion program.

SETTING REALISTIC GOALS

No matter what size your office is, you should be able to establish realistic, measurable goals, like getting three new packaging projects this year, or five additional clients, or two more annual report assignments. Short-term, this translates into a series of daily marketing actions. For example, as you read the business section of your local newspaper, clip articles about newly appointed executives in regional companies who sound like promising potential clients. Every week send out four or five of your capabilities brochures introducing new prospects to your services. Don't just mail the brochure in an envelope, but enclose a cover letter addressed to the prospect. For example; "Congratulations on your recent appointment as Marketing Director for The X Corporation...". Follow this up by calling within a week to ask the recipient to if he has seen the brochure, describe how you can be of benefit his company, and request an opportunity to personally show him your firm's work. The goal here is not to sell your services on the phone, but to get a sales call appointment.

DELEGATING IN-HOUSE MARKETING SUPPORT

The principal of a small office assumes many roles in managing the business. Priority is obviously given to the job and client of the moment and new business development is neglected or handled indifferently. Make better use of your receptionist/secretary and staff or hire a part-time person to assume the following responsibilities:

Market Research Assistant: Makes cold calls to qualify and update mailing list, and enters information in database

Promotion Coordinator: Implements marketing strategies, prepares all direct mail materials

Office Archivist/Librarian: Organizes and maintains the file of slides and printed samples. Handles competition entry forms and mailings

For the larger design office, periodic mailings are only part of the total marketing and promotion program. Not only will the principal(s) of the firm be directly involved in making client presentations, but if there is a marketing support person on staff, the program will be able to include additional outreach efforts to create greater visibility for the firm, such as speaking engagements, articles in local papers, and pro bono participation in a few choice nonprofit organizations. Self-promotion includes the designer with the design . . . creating an awareness of the personality, intelligence and credibility of the person as well as his firm.

NEW BUSINESS, PROMOTION, SALES = MARKETING

As a consultant and journalist, I frequently have the opportunity to interview a wide range of designers to find out how they market their company. Occasionally one will tell me, "We don't have a marketing plan," or "We don't (need to) market our services," implying that marketing is some kind of embarrassing, desperate activity rather than a necessary and accepted professional practice. Marketing, promotion and sales are fundamental to every business and anyone who says that they do not have to make any effort in these areas is either not honest or not in business. Designers do not always realize that many things they do instinctively to get new business count as "marketing" even though they may not have any formal program in operation. Calling existing clients and casually asking, "Hi. What's happening?" is a sales call, and sending a calendar or Christmas card is promotion, and so is the business lunch.

KEEPING A HIGH PROFILE

Any activity that promotes interest in yourself as an authority on effective communication design is considered marketing. Your primary goal is to translate this attention into new business. Many designers have the gift of speaking well and are articulate representatives of the profession. You will find them on the list of featured speakers at design conferences and seminars throughout the country. While this outlet provides healthy ego-reinforcement and is usually of interest to other designers and students, it does nothing to build a relationship with the client side, your market. Designers frequently complain that clients do not understand or appreciate good work and are not willing to pay for quality design. It is time to realize that speaking exclusively to other designers will not improve this situation, so get out and speak in the business community at every opportunity. It will not only enrich your own practice, it will do a great deal to promote understanding and respect for good design in general. Reaching out to connect with the world of business is personally and professionally validating, an educational experience for both designer and client. Take advantage of every chance to promote discussions about successful design case studies and

Reaching out to connect with the world of business is an educational experience for both designer and client.

encourage client side participation. The best design is the result of a strong mutual partnership. If you do not have access to or find no interesting opportunities, initiate your own programs by inviting a selected group of business guests to your office for a design seminar or workshop, and consider including them in your local design association panel discussions. The benefits from this kind of "cultural exchange" are exceptional. By taking the initiative to organize such events you have positioned yourself as an expert design consultant, not simply a "vendor."

WORKING PRO BONO

Pro bono activities are an excellent way to introduce yourself to the community. When I was an account executive for a Los Angeles design firm, I observed that some of our best clients were also involved in the local art world as collectors, contributors and museum board members. By becoming more involved in this mutually interesting arena, we would be able to position ourselves as peers and take existing relationships to a deeper level. Our office volunteered to design the poster and invitation for the Venice Family Clinic's prestigious annual ArtWalk. This successful charity event gave us new access and visibility. As a result of this exposure we were subsequently hired to design the catalog for an important corporate art collection gallery. A note of caution regarding "pro bono" (from the Latin pro bono publico): working for free does not make the working relationship simple or guarantee that your generosity is always appreciated. Often these jobs are more stressful and demanding than paying ones. At the outset of the project make it very clear in writing what you will and will not provide. Out-of-pocket expenses like messengers, film, film processing and printing are to be paid by the client. Your office staff cannot be expected to be at the disposal of the client organization to respond to their daily emergency phone calls. Delegate one person as the contact person for the job.

Proofreading is not your responsibility. Changes must be in writing and signed off on. Although you are donating your time, keep track of the time spent on the job—it will be useful later; ask your accountant. Most likely you will be working with non-professionals who do not always understand business procedures. Be gracious, be cooperative, but be firm.

USING YOUR WRITING SKILLS

If your writing skill is more compelling than your performance talent, make use of this to establish your firm's visibility in the form of letters, newsletters, press releases, and newspaper and magazine articles. You are free to express yourself on any subject, from money-saving production tips, successful case studies of recent projects, or future trends in your special design area. Although obviously these are self-promotion vehicles, give the reader something of real interest and relevance, an article worth saving that speaks to his own marketing communication needs. You will have his attention for a very short time, so don't waste this opportunity.

BUILDING YOUR REPUTATION: BE AVAILABLE

In addition to the self-generated publicity that I have just described, let me discuss a strange situation that I am dealing with at the moment. Preparing for a new story that I am writing for a well-known design magazine, I have sent out letters and research questionnaires to over a dozen designers asking for their participation. I need six interviewees for the article, who will show examples of their work as well as a picture of themselves. There is no cost to them other than the time it will take to answer the questions and the cost of mailing the photo and slides. You may assume, as I did, that designers would consider this a great opportunity to discuss issues and get their recent work in print. Not necessarily. I find it quite difficult to get this kind of cooperation and involvement. Of the total number I contacted in the past month, only three have told me they will participate. If you have wondered why you keep reading about the same group of "hot" designers, one of the reasons is that these people are accessible and willing. They are also ready with good photographs of themselves and their latest work on file. Smart designers know that a reprint of a magazine or newspaper article featuring them gives immediate credibility and makes an excellent promotional piece, so be available and be prepared.

COMMUNICATION AND NEW MEDIA TECHNOLOGY

A note on technology. I am not a cyberwizard, and even if I were, electronic technology is progressing so rapidly that no one can guarantee what the most prevailing interactive communication tool will be in the future. As a member of the digital age you will certainly want to take advantage of the growing power of the Internet and other new media networks to improve your business performance. As you step boldly into cyberspace, remember that your competitive advantage will come from your ability to get your message noticed and retained above the thousands of other sites. This requires intelligent copy, well-executed, accessible design and, especially important, the ability of your office to respond quickly to prospects' inquiries. Whatever the medium of communication, it will always be a matter of getting the message (product) into the marketplace and making a connection (sale). The decision to hire your firm ultimately still depends on the relationship between two live human beings. Don't be seduced by technology.

CONSIDERATE SELF-PROMOTION

The self-promotion program of a design firm can be elaborate and time-consuming or straightforward and efficient. Some offices seem to produce an endless series of mailings followed up by too many eager, cheerful calls and letters. It is possible to overdo self-promotion, so be considerate. Every message from your office should have a valid reason for being sent—an outstanding project, an important new client or a recent design award, for example. Stay flexible enough to allow for unexpected good news or changes within your office. The most important thing to remember is whatever you decide to do, don't give up after the first mailing if you don't get the enthusiastic response you anticipated. Remain committed to continuing your program. Remember that prospective client I cited who said she received a terrific brochure from a design firm, saved it, and never heard from them again. You can't always expect the prospect to act on their interest by contacting you. Follow up. Follow up. Follow up.

Every message from your office should have a valid reason for being sent.

THE DESIGN MARKETING ROAD MAP

The following outlines a typical design marketing and promotion program.

Establish a Database

100 to 200 prospect companies, to update and add to regularly

Create the Mailing List, to contain;

Contact names, title, address, telephone, fax, E-mail address

Existing clients, prospects, vendors, suppliers, media

A regularly updated list of your ten most wanted clients

Develop a Tracking System

Keep a record of all marketing and promotional activities including:

Mailings: date, number sent out, responses

Sales presentation meetings: report of meeting results, suggestions for future improvements

Prospective client data: note all important information relating to future opportunities to recontact such as trade organization membership, meeting dates

Speeches and seminars

Exhibits/trade shows

Events/parties

Establish a Research File

A collection of related information on prospective client companies and industry trends, news

Build an Office Capabilities and Promotion Materials Library

Your complete graphics identity system (stationery, forms, labels, folders, mailing supplies)

Capabilities brochure or equivalent

Form letters/proposal form

Client and project list

List of client references

List of design awards

Samples of design projects

Newsletters

Media articles

Direct mail pieces

Reprints, design books

Press releases

Advertising copy, layouts

Audiovisual support; slides, video, CD-ROM

Website presentation

Special occasion promotions such as holiday greeting cards, calendars, moving announcements, party invitations, posters

Holiday and gift specialties, T-shirts, handmade one-offs

ESTABLISHING A MARKETING BUDGET

Establishing the budget for your marketing and self-promotion activities is an individual decision. The creativity of the idea does not necessarily depend on the production cost. Often highly original ideas are produced for little more than postage and time. The business-dictated rule suggests that an average of 7-15% of your gross revenues be allotted for your marketing program, but some offices spend much more than this and some much less. This should be planned in advance. At the beginning of your Marketing Calendar, estimate what each project will cost in terms of cash outlay and number of hours. Make every effort to stay on schedule, take production and mailing deadlines seriously and keep them. If you spend many hours of your own and your staff's time hand-assembling promotional pieces, does this count, and should it be "billed" at your regular hourly rate? Technically, yes. Although these projects are fun and budgets are often forgotten when the Santa's workshop mood overcomes the office, the bottom line is still sales, not simply good will. The criteria for the holiday gift should be that it is appropriate to your business and useful to the recipient. As delighted as your clients may be with your clever Christmas present, will this result in new business? If you spend your whole budget in December, will they remember you in July? How can you maintain a continuous, effective marketing program throughout the year? It costs money to make money, as they say, but spend it wisely.

An additional note . . . if you don't have a great idea this year, don't send out a mediocre one. It can do you more harm than good to mail a hastily produced, trite concept. It is perfectly acceptable to send a simple card that announces that this year your office will make a contribution to a favorite charity in lieu of a holiday promotion. In the season of excess, this sincere gesture may stand out more than an extravagant display.

If you spend your whole budget in December, will they remember you in July?

BUSINESS ENTERTAINMENT

You may not think of business entertainment, including office parties, as promotion, but in a professional context it's hard to separate the business from the entertainment. It is a party at your workplace, you have invited clients, colleagues and vendors for an occasion that provides an agreeable setting for exchanging information, making new contacts and generally promoting good will and fun. What can you expect to gain from this event? The first question to ask after the party is, "Of those people invited, who came?" Like any other mailing, you want to know your rate of return. A good, unobtrusive way to find out is to hold a business card drawing for a door prize; now you have a record of your guests. Not every party has to include your entire mailing list; sometimes a smaller, select group is better.

I once planned a dinner party held at our office for a group of ten women executives. Some of them were already clients; the rest were desirable prospects. The designer and I felt that this group of smart, accomplished women were special and rare, deserving of the "endangered species" treatment, so this became the theme of the party. We had fun developing this concept. The invitations were available cards that featured a series of photographs of endangered wild animals, the decorations included a tablecloth made from a zebra-printed bed sheet, a tent-like mosquito net over the table, and oil-burning lamps for ambient light. Slides of jungle creatures were projected on one wall and a recorded tape of jungle sounds provided an appropriate wild note. Each guest received a leopard-printed cap with our logo patch. The evening was a great success, everyone enjoyed this informal gathering of peers and was delighted by the humor and creativity displayed, including the meal, which was prepared by the hostess designer. Being hospitable on your own turf rather than at a restaurant, is economical and out of the ordinary . . . which is how you want to be perceived. So, if you are a great cook and love to entertain, consider self promotion at the table.

IMAGINATION AND SELF-PROMOTION

Your gift mailing can showcase your office's creativity in ways that can suggest new design capabilities to add to your list of services. For example, publication designer, Beth Tondreau, BTD, in New York, has a special flair for sophisticated packaging and sends her clients appealing holiday presents, among them a candle-making kit, a set of exotic tea bags and even her own micro-brewed beer. She hopes that these projects will attract new design assignments from an entirely different clientele than those she now represents, thus expanding and diversifying her practice. (*See Chapter 8 pages 104-106.*)

It is not mandatory for you to do a holiday mailing, but the Christmas and New Year season has an expansive, playful mood and often there is some office downtime. Promotional projects are times for the whole staff to work together and this arts-and-crafts exercise builds teamwork and camaraderie.

Holiday spirit can take many different forms from elegant gourmet treats to simple, thoughtful gifts. In Wichita, Kansas, the Gretman Design Group made a substantial donation on their client's behalf to a program that provided energy assistance to the elderly and severely disabled. To convey the message they developed a theme, "Light the Night," including an aromatic candle, customized box of matches and a card. One hundred fifty pieces were hand-delivered or mailed. The response to this gesture was overwhelmingly positive. What a sincere, compassionate way to state the values of this design firm. (*See page 112.*)

One of my clients, Michael Boland of Watts Design? Inc. in lower Manhattan, has a small, informal office whose most conspicuous member is a spotted white boxer named Cookie. While office dogs are not that remarkable, she is a distinctive-looking pet who adds a special touch to this workplace. "Why not include Cookie in some of the firm's promotions?" I suggested. My rationale was that Cookie could contribute her memorable personality to the firm and prospective clients would surely remember

Watts Design? and its spotted dog. In the same way, another firm might feature their striking office design or off-beat location as a distinguishing feature. Although marketing consultants can suggest, recommend or strongly advise, we can't force something to be done, so after a year, I was a little disappointed that my strategy had not yet been tested. A few weeks ago I received an invitation to a party at their new office space. There was Cookie on the front of the card with "Please pull tongue" and the new address printed there. "This card certainly got a laugh," Michael said; "Now that we've gotten past the first few tough years in business, we can relax and show our sense of humor."

The best self-promotions start with a strong idea, followed by smart copy and a design concept as well-conceived as the work you do for your best clients. Too many of the promotional pieces I see have all the right elements except one . . . a return address and telephone number! It is surprisingly easy to overlook this most basic information, but without it, what's the point? Even Web sites can fail to provide contact information or make it very obscure. Make sure your street and E-mail addresses, Web site, telephone and fax numbers are easily found. Have your copy proofread at least twice before printing. Assume nothing.

THE DIFFERENCE BETWEEN MARKETING AND SELF-PROMOTION

These two terms are often confused and used interchangeably, but although they are interrelated, they are not the same. Basically, marketing refers to the process of finding, creating, attracting and satisfying the client. This process, as I continue to emphasize, is constant and not limited to an annual calendar or quarterly mailings. Every single conscious or spontaneous thing you do to find and keep business is marketing.

Self-promotion is one of a number of tools employed to introduce you to the marketplace and maintain an ongoing aware-

Every single conscious or spontaneous thing you do to find and keep business is marketing.

ness of your company's name and work. It takes many forms, from the mailing of your latest capabilities brochure to speaking at the local Chamber of Commerce meeting. Although you are clearly promoting your own office, it is equally important to remember that you are representing the design profession as a whole. To quote the wise ad line from a Manhattan retailer, "An educated consumer is the best customer."

Self-promotion is just as significant, sometimes more, than whatever client project you are working on at the moment. Your own marketing program is the easiest thing to neglect or postpone but without marketing, new business is difficult to find and old business hard to keep. It takes planning, time and a lot of patience. Like growing a garden, you can't enjoy the harvest without planting the seeds and tending the crop.

CHAPTER 8

SUCCESSFUL MARKETING PROGRAMS

One day a prospective client receives a T-shirt in the mail. Although, like most of us, she has plenty of other T-shirts, this one is really fun, the design is bold and attracts compliments from people. "Where did you get that great T-shirt?" they ask. She can't help noticing that the design on the shirt is much better than the others she wears and realizes, subliminally perhaps, that if this design firm has attracted so much positive attention with a T-shirt, what would they be like to work with? Fun? What kinds of projects have they done? Look at that brochure they sent recently. Who are their clients? That information is on the letter that was sent with the brochure, and a press release that she will receive next month describes a new job for a prominent local company. So the shirt by itself is not a marketing program, but is an appealing element in the whole new business development process. The T-shirt, which has become almost an international form of currency, may not continue to be such a great promotional idea, but something else will come along to take its place. Watch for the next trend to become a new vehicle for your firm's message.

The following examples of self-promotional materials range from low-cost, handmade pieces to elaborate gifts and four-color brochures. They are effective, not only because of the quality of the design, but are representative of successful elements in ongoing marketing programs. None of these firms depends on a single mailing to generate new business.

The designers here not only show their creative imagination, but use these promotional pieces to express the spirit and personality of the firm, showing not only what they do but who they are. This work immediately engages the attention of the recipient, conveys a strong message and often reveals something about the culture and values of the firm.

The purpose of self promotion is not only to attract new clients, but is a way to stay in touch with existing ones. "Customer retention" is one of the key rules of business that certainly applies to the design business.

SUCCESSFUL SELF-PROMOTION PROJECTS

No matter what a design firm's size or budget, a consistent, memorable marketing and self-promotion program is vitally important to the business.

BTD
Beth Tondreau
New York City

BTD is a small, "boutique" design office with a client base consisting primarily of high-end book publishers. For an office her size, Tondreau invests a considerable amount of her budget on self promotion, 10-25%. With a mailing list of 250, she estimates the average cost of producing each of the mailings shown here at $8,000, with the T-Shirt coming in at $15,000. Each year's promotion results in one or two new clients. Of equal importance to Tondreau is the fact that these promotions help to maintain a connection with existing clients and increase awareness of the office's broader range of talents. "Because the bulk of our work is in print, 'marketing toys' enable us to show abilities in other areas. Working on promos also gives everyone here a morale boost with a good team project."

BTD BUSINESS CARD: A MARKETING OPPORTUNITY

Within the standard business card size, BTD manages to create a three-panel, two-sided mini-brochure, showing three projects, and a capabilities list in addition to the usual information.

BEE TEE BAGS

"We attached customized tags to tea bags and inserted them into a slit in our holiday card. Our copy, "As you rush about during the holidays, relax a moment with a soothing cup-o-B Tea."

CANDLE-MAKING KIT

"For a selected group of clients, we mailed a holiday candle-making kit consisting of two sheets of beeswax, two wicks, illustrative instructions for "rolling your own" candle, and matchboxes with the line, "Illuminating Design." The theme, printed on an enclosed bookmark, is a quote by Jonathan Swift:

"Instead of dirt and poison we have rather chosen to fill our hives with honey and wax, thus furnishing mankind with the two noblest of things, which are sweetness and light."

10TH ANNIVERSARY BEE TEE SHIRT

"I wanted to commemorate ten years in business, thank our clients, and work with both paper and other materials to demonstrate that we work in media other than print. A simple folder opens to reveal an oversized T-shirt with our Bee silk-screened on the sleeve. We had a phenomenal response, receiving calls and letters thanking us and praising our work; recipients even sent photographs of themselves wearing the shirts."

All BTD photo credits: Steven Mays

UP Design
Gary Underhill and Wendy Peters, Partners
Montclair, New Jersey

UP Design is a young husband-and-wife team whose serious investment in marketing their design firm is expressed in long overtime hours rather than in dollars. "The most expensive part of our promotional program is the postage. We really try to do everything for as little as possible. By using our laser printer and paper samples, and assembling by hand, we save a lot of money. When we need to print something we barter with a local printer."

UP Design tries for a balance between a handmade look and professionally printed pieces, and with cost not a major factor, they can afford to contact clients and prospects frequently. The average unit cost of a vacation announcement is $1.75, including postage. In addition to their Christmas mailing and July vacation closing announcement, they send either a press release, their UP DATE booklet newsletter, or a sample a of special client project every 30-45 days. The present mailing list of 150 to 250 names includes current clients, prospects, vendors and media, with ongoing research of potential clients. A good idea: most of their major mailings include a response reply card.

SUMMER VACATION ANNOUNCEMENT

Office closing days have been added to the UP logo printed on a beach ball. Deflated ball is folded and shipped in a standard square packing box used to ship all promotional items.

HOLIDAY CARD WITH GIFT TAGS

This greeting card also served as the holiday office closing announcement and included a set of Christmas gift tags. The print cost was bartered, as the same tag designs were used by the printing company.

UP DATE BOOKLETS

UP DATE is a handmade, inexpensive to produce, booklet to keep current clients informed of recent projects. It's printed using the office laser printer on available paper samples.

PARTY INVITATION

This office open house invitation became the standard UP format for all fun mailings in their little square box.

DSI/LA
Rod Parker, Principal
Baton Rouge, Louisiana

DSI/LA is a 24-person design and advertising company with clients primarily in the corporate and financial services areas. A full-time business development director oversees their capabilities mailings, including two case studies every six weeks to targeted prospects, a semi-annual overview of recent work, plus Thanksgiving and Christmas cards. Occasionally they send out homemade "designer" Christmas gifts. Although DSI/LA has a database of 1,200 clients and key prospects, they rarely mail to all of them. Despite its location in what is considered the languorous Deep South, DSI/LA maintains an aggressive marketing and promotion campaign. With emphasis on strong concept and copy, the firm's self-promotion demonstrates good design and creative thinking at work and play.

WEBSITE ANNOUNCEMENT

To let people know that they are now "surf-able," the card's message reads, "We've always had vision, now we have site."

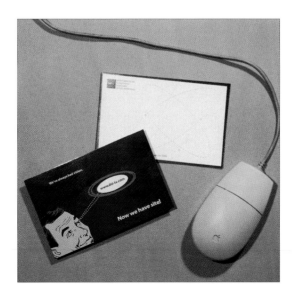

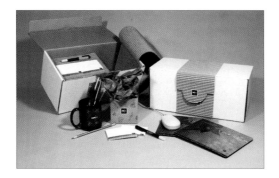

DESK ACCESSORY KIT
Seeking a unique container for a gift pack, DSI/LA opted for a handmade solution. The kit, given only to new clients whose billing is more than $25,000 in fees, contains a DSI/LA mouse pad, pens, pencils, highlighters, Post-it notes and a desktop perpetual calendar. When appropriate, the capabilities brochure is enclosed with the cover letter.

HUNGRY POSTCARD
"Survival of the fittest" is the theme of this alarming image; a montage of bugs, the urban jungle and a sandwich. The copy on the reverse side poses direct questions and invites the prospect for a portfolio tour.

MOVING ANNOUNCEMENT
An office relocation always presents a creative challenge. DIS/LA's short move from an office park to a bank building inspired this

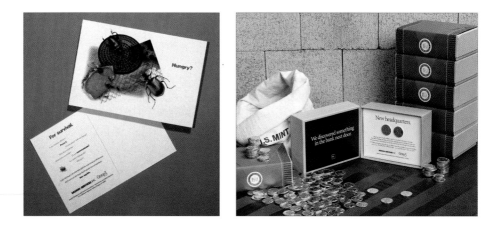

idea for a mailer with a coin wrapper-like exterior and uncirculated new quarters, heads up, of course.

Parker estimates that the ongoing capabilities program averages $650 per month not including labor. Last year his out-of-pocket cost for all marketing and promotional activities was $32,000. About 5% of his overhead is spent on these activities, $18, 000–20,000 per million dollars in sales. As a direct result of promotional mailings, DSI/LA averages three to six new clients a year. "We practice what we preach," says Parker. "No one can see the value in good design if we don't value it ourselves. DSI/LA is proof that marketing works. While we don't want to intrude on people's lives with unwanted sales calls, we don't want them to forget about us either. Landing a half-million dollar job as a result of keeping in touch with a prospect thousands of miles away convinced us that promotional efforts pay off. The other benefit is an internal one. Presenting ourselves keeps everyone in the company focused on our mutual objectives."

Gretman Design Group
Sonia Gretman
Wichita, Kansas

Two examples of creative self-promotional tools from this small firm show that a well-conceived idea and strategic targeting are key to the success of each program. Departing from their usual gift-giving tradition, the Gretman Group made a substantial donation on their clients' behalf to a local program that provides energy assistance to senior citizens and the severely disabled. The small present sent to convey the message of the theme, "Light the Night," was a small aromatic candle in a tin with a two-color, kraft paper label. Also enclosed was a custom box of matches and a card. One hundred fifty sets were hand-delivered or mailed to clients and key contacts. Cost: approximately $15 each.

CHRISTMAS MAILING: "LIGHT THE NIGHT"

GRETMAN GROUP PORTFOLIO

Using an unconventional size proved efficient and cost-effective for this capabilities piece. Two small, hand-assembled, spiral-bound books within a portfolio folder offer a quick, yet comprehensive overview of the group's work. The use of cardboard, corrugated material and metal elements for the covers create the highly tactile feeling of packaging, one of the firm's special areas of expertise. One book features corporate identity projects, the other provides samples of a wide range of design capabilities from signage to Websites.

The portfolio is custom-assembled to prospective clients as needed. The average cost per portfolio is approximately $30 and is more than justified by the positive responses received.

While Gretman won't go so far as to claim that mailing one of the portfolios guarantees immediate new business, she is convinced that it is a key part of the total marketing program.

Communication Arts, Inc.
Janet Martin, President
Boulder, Colorado

One might think that a large 24-year-old design office would be so well established that marketing is not as necessary as it would be for a young and hungry office. Not true. Keeping a staff of 50 busy requires a lot of projects and Boulder is not exactly the hub of the universe. Martin believes that marketing has been important to the success of the practice because it allows the firm to stay in touch. CommArts has a mailing list of 2,500 and allocates 7% of its income for marketing and promotion. Although the number of new clients acquired as a direct result of these efforts is only 1%, Martin stresses that creating fresh relationships with existing clients and their business developments is equally important. "We are able to transfer what we have learned in one area of our work, like retailing, and apply this to something new for us, like resorts. Our business is mostly through referral, so our best marketing is the work we produce."

INTEROFFICE PROMOTIONS

In addition to appealing to present and future clients with examples of completed projects, CommArts promotes itself from within, by acknowledging employees' career advancements. Announcements of staff promotions are proudly mailed to clients, stressing that individual success in the office is a direct result of the success of the projects.

INVITATIONS, ANNUAL HOLIDAY PARTY

The yearly holiday party is just one of many activities sponsored by CommArts for its employees. A group of employees is selected to plan the party as well as design the invitation. The graphics express the fun and esprit de corps, which is the purpose of these events.

AdamsMorioka
Sean Adams, and Noreen Morioka, Partners
Beverly Hills, California

This-five-person office is very much about personality and visibility. Adams and Morioka clearly enjoy marketing and promotion. It gives them the opportunity to interface with new client contacts and keeps the practice fresh by introducing new challenges and strategies. They budget: 5% of their income for marketing, with a mailing list of 1,000 to 15,000. The marketing approach of this office is simple: a series of postcards, seasonal gifts or limited-edition posters.

"We are true believers in direct contact and building new business through existing clients. Our marketing plan is word-of-mouth, networking and actual, in-the-flesh contact. We rarely produce direct mail pieces or mass mailings. Our work has been published often in both design and mainstream publications, and we frequently accept speaking engagements. While we are not sure whether published work or lectures contribute directly to new business development, the indirect benefit is a greater presence. This gives us a higher level of credibility which helps us in a competitive market."

Adams and Morioka, who work in the image-conscious environment of Beverly Hills, are not shy about introducing themselves as the product in these engaging postcards. Such a bold approach may not be not for everyone, but it works for these two designer-extroverts.

Photo credits: Blake Little, Penny Wolin, various

"Better Quality, Better Price"
"America's Favorite"
"We're Here. #1"
"We're Here. #2"

Platinum Design, Inc.
Vickie Peslak, President
New York, New York

Platinum Design has been doing business in New York City, The Land of the Bottomless Hustle, for 12 years. Its latest efforts are focused on creating a new company image and Web presence. A small firm with a sophisticated outlook, Peslak wants to reflect a classic approach to design without bowing to current trends. "Marketing in a highly competitive environment is important, both enjoyable and a chore simultaneously, but it's necessary to our success." Without committing a specific amount to the annual marketing budget, Peslak believes firmly in spending whatever is needed at the time to get the firm's name out on a regular basis. With a mailing list of about 3,000, the studio manager at Platinum is responsible for good tracking, record-keeping and reviewing.

PROMOTIONAL BROCHURE

Platinum needed a capabilities brochure to send to prospective clients and to use as a leave-behind. The goal for this piece was to show the work at its best, be easily accessible, flexible, and small enough to keep but large enough to make a good impression. The wire binding allows each brochure to be custom-bound for each situation. Cost: approximately $20 each. Quantity: 1,000

PLATINUM WEBSITE

Science Theme: The Periodical Table of the Elements
The firm wanted to use the Worldwide Web as a marketing vehicle to reach an unlimited number of prospective clients throughout the U.S. and possibly the world. The website allows viewers who might not have heard of Platinum Design otherwise to access the portfolio and serves as a showcase for Platinum's multimedia design capability. The four segments are the firm's biography, client list, portfolio and contact page. In order to allow for fast downloading and easy navigation,  the site has been designed with a limited use of color and selective application of animation and photography. Platinum is enthusiastic about the results so far with this latest marketing tool.

Sayles Graphic Design
John Sayles and Sheree Clark, Partners
Des Moines, Iowa

In the realm of self-promotion, I have the feeling that there isn't anything that Sheree Clark has not tried on behalf of Sayles Graphic Design. She is the most tireless marketeer I know. Her energy would not be unappreciated in any big city firm, but the fact that she has been successful in building a small design office located in Des Moines, Iowa, is truly outstanding. With partner John Sayles, she has made everything about their company and lifestyle part of their promotional campaign, using their house, built in the 1930s, and art deco collection of furnishings, as an additional way to distinguish themselves. Sayles has a bold, distinctive style that is immediately recognizable, and by aggressively marketing their work, they have successfully reached new clients throughout the country, well beyond the state line. The company's many design awards keep them involved and visible.

Clark explains that although they do not have a formal marketing "plan," they employ a flexible, responsive strategy that changes with their needs. A budget for marketing and promotion is not based on a percentage of their income, but is determined by what they think is necessary or appropriate at the time. The average cost per unit ranges from $2 to $12.

T-SHIRT: "CUTTING EDGE"
The back of the shirt shows a typical Sayles figure carrying a giant X-Acto knife. One of a series of collectible, wearable promotions.

POSTERS: "TOP OF THE THIRD"

A baseball theme used for a larger-than-life poster celebrating the firm's third anniversary. Screen printed in three colors on 60″ x 22″ corrugated stock, it announces, "It's a hit!"

"HIGH FIVE"

A single bold graphic for their fifth anniversary featuring Sayles'
hand-rendered visual and type screen printed in red on black
paper. A limited run of 200 was produced.

MAILER: "PERFECT MATCH"

Designed just to keep their name out there, this says that Sayles Graphic Design is a "perfect match" for potential clients. The 4″ x 5″ foldout format includes a business reply card.

Williams and House
Pam Williams, Partner
Avon, Connecticut

"Self-promotion gives us the opportunity to demonstrate in a tangible way the values we find important: great thinking, attention to detail, personalized communication and friendly relationships. Our pieces tend to be personal, substantial and useful in nature, and we send only to clients, friends and suppliers, not prospects. Since 99% of our business is by referral, we want to stay "top-of-the mind." As a company of eight people, we get together and do much of the handwork ourselves. It gives us time to enjoy each other's company outside of the day-to-day routine; we wouldn't do this if we didn't enjoy it."

HOLIDAY GREETING/ THE HOLIDAY GRIND

Williams and House is known among their friends and clients for their love of great food and good coffee. Each of the 300 packages include three samples of flavored coffees and a cookbook featuring favorite dessert recipes from each member of the office, and the purple packing material was even shredded in their own shredder. For the past two years the Williams and House holiday gift has been a package of 24 engraved cards.

MULTI-OCCASION GREETING CARD SET

The response to the previous year's greeting card gift set was so enthusiastic that the firm topped it the following season with a series of 5¼ " x 4" deckle-edged note cards with a custom-engraved vellum wrap and silver ink pen to express the importance the firm places on saying "Thank you" to friends and clients.

VALENTINE GREETING

This unusual hand-assembled Valentine's Day card was designed to convey the greeting of the day as well as use up hundreds of extra pink and white striped paper clips left over from a previous project.

Photo credit: Mark Brendel, Ulsaker Studio

CINCO DE MAYO
T-SHIRT GIVEAWAY

The art from the Invitation Poster is repeated on a gift T-shirt and packed in a brown paper tote bag.

Mark Oliver, Inc.
Mark Oliver, President
Santa Barbara, California

MOI is a brand consultancy, primarily creating package design for food and beverage manufacturers. Because of this specialized market, the firm needed a standout method to show their work to prospective clients.

Photo credit: Greg Voight

MARK OLIVER, INC. CAPABILITIES BROCHURE

"Our objective was to create a cost-effective, easy-to-fabricate self-promotion piece that would allow us to easily update material, customize according to prospect, and be unique. The solution is this fan book—the same concept as a color swatch book—consisting of kraft cardboard covers with a series of full-color inserts held with a nylon screw-type fastener. Cover art consists of common packaging images such as bar codes, recycling symbols etc., to immediately express what this brochure is about. The brochure is mailed with a cover letter in a Oliver-designed box that seals tightly and requires no tape or adhesives."

MOI BROCHURE: INSERT PAGES

Insert pages are printed on coated cover-weight stock on one side. Each page is devoted to a single client project, including a photograph of the project and a brief case history: problem, concept, solution and resulting change in sales, if possible. Initial print run 2,500. Current brochure is 28 pages.

SAMPLES OF OTHER MOI BROCHURES:

Using the same format and materials now associated with the firm, the designer has created additional promotional pieces highlighting new clients and projects. Because the size is the same as the main brochure, these inserts will eventually become merged into future capabilities mailings. There are two or three promotional mailings a year to a list of 1,500.

Oliver tells me that the results from this program have been more than satisfactory. Believe it or not, prospects even call and ask to be put on the mailing list. The "fan book" is remembered and kept. Follow-up phone calls after mailings allow him to track new clients and study the results of his efforts. "Our self-promotion package works well because it is very focused. Packaging is a promise. Everyone wants to see what is inside of a package. What better way to promote what we do?"

Lambert Design
Christie Lambert Rasmussen, President
Dallas, Texas

"In marketing our studio, we feel that continual self-promotion is mandatory, and we are always trying to come up with clever ways to keep our name in front of our clients."

In addition to the one or two promotional pieces a year, Lambert Design donates design services to a local charity and helps vendors with free projects in exchange for design credit. Their favorite promotion is the annual holiday piece, and by hand-delivering each one, when possible, they can keep costs down and personally visit with clients and vendors. Some of the holiday gifts incorporate client products. For Lambert Design, the holiday promotion is a "thank you for your support" message.

The average cost per unit ranges from $5 to $15 and the mailing list is limited to around 200. By constantly updating their list, they are able to include a few new names as well as focus on keeping current clients happy. The better the business year, the better the gift!

CHRISTMAS WRAPPING PAPER

Defining the spirit of the giving season, Lambert Design selected The Family Place, a women's shelter for victims of domestic

violence. Drawings made by some of the residents were used on the gift wrap paper, which was sent with a poem and a request for clients to wrap a gift to send to the shelter during the holiday season.

Printing was donated; the cost per unit, including mailing, was $4. The response was overwhelmingly positive, and in addition to winning several awards, the office picked up two new clients.

LUCKY-P-RANCH

In the Southwest, it is traditional to eat black-eyed peas on New Year's Day for good luck in the coming year. The objective was to attract attention with a fun idea. The pea package included a recipe for good luck. Quantity: 100, cost per unit $6. Bonus: one new packaging client.

BAG-IT OPEN HOUSE

Working again with The Family Place Shelter, the studio invited clients to fill the bag with items for the shelter residents and bring it to an open house party at the office. The printing was donated, and the cost of the mailing was $1.50... the party cost a lot more.

Clients came to the party, personally met the staff, some for the first time, and saw the studio as more than simply a design business. The benefit of such community outreach work, is that it positions the studio as special by revealing generosity and humanity in addition to creativity.

Vaughn Wedeen Creative, Inc.
Rick Vaughn, Steve Wedeen,
Richard Kuhn, Partners
Albuquerque, New Mexico

"The heart of our holiday promotion is the desire to share a little bit of ourselves and our surroundings with our clients, vendors and friends, most of whom live outside of New Mexico," says Steve Wedeen. These promotional gifts frequently serve to showcase their appealing style. For Vaughn Wedeen, a good-sized firm in a sparsely populated state, these mailings are a pleasing way of extending their hospitality and pride of place beyond their immediate surroundings. These promotions also introduce the staff designers to the clients in a more personal way, whether it's simply a matter of sending out their homemade cookies or showing what they can create from a can of assorted "found" pieces, "GIZMO." Consistent with the rest of their marketing materials, the promotions express the office as a talented, friendly and accessible group of individuals.

UNIQUE NEW MEXICAN TREATS
The wooden gift crate contains an assortment of regional specialties: Red Chile Jelly, Green Chile Salsa and Blue Corn Tortilla Chips.

CHRISTMAS COOKIES

This year the tradition of sending food items to clients became more personal. Each member of the studio staff baked cookies from their favorite recipes. The cookies were packed in an attractive tin, sharing the recipe and a small story about its significance to the maker.

"GIZMO"

Moving away from edibles the following season, Vaughn Wedeen created a build-it-yourself toy called "Gizmo" consisting of 125 "found" pieces selected primarily for their visual appeal. Staff members built creations which were photographed and shown in an enclosed booklet with a story about each. Recipients were invited to send pictures of their own toy creations. "Gizmo" was meant to encourage clients and friends to express their own creative talents.

The DePuis Group
Steven DePuis, Principal
Woodland Hills, California

"Our direct mail campaign consists of eight 6″x 9″ cards. Each one showcases a recent project or program. The copy on the back gives detailed information about the results of the project to support our claim, 'Designs that sell'," explains DePuis. This firm has reduced self-promotion to a very simple system that reinforces the message that good design is an effective, measurable element. The image of the company is very businesslike and direct, no games, no T-shirts. This marketing system is appropriate for them and demonstrates that a straightforward approach, aggressively applied, can be very successful.

THE KEYSTONE OF MARKETING AND DESIGN
Expresses the DePuis Group positioning philosophy. Copy on reverse side provides contact information and describes services.

THE DEPUIS GROUP CARD SERIES

Printed eight-up and UV-coated. The cost to print 1,500, including photography: $10,000.

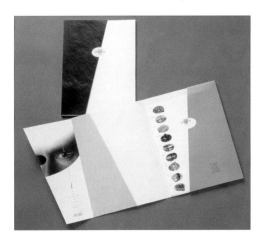

INTRODUCTORY FOLDER

Depending on the recipient, it can contain samples and marketing one-sheets or proposals and contracts. The piece was printed on matte stock with metallic inks. Die cut in right-hand pocket shows DePuis logo. Cost of producing 1,000 folders: $15,000.

Vrontikis Design Office
Petrula Vrontikis, Principal
Los Angeles, California

When asked about how she markets her company, Vrontikis explains, "Years ago, I had a larger studio and a business manager. We had a marketing plan that was very time-consuming and not as successful as we'd hoped. The work that did come in barely covered the time to implement and maintain the plan. The best, most profitable work was still coming from existing and referral clients. Now that my studio is small, a formal plan is unnecessary, and projects are more profitable. At present all of my new work comes from word-of-mouth, mainly referrals from great clients, and vendors like printing and paper reps. Being published in international design books and magazines has also brought a lot of work in. I'm surprised at the number of clients who browse

HOLIDAY
GIFTTAG COLLECTIONS

those sources. In addition, people I've met through my teaching position at the Art Center have led to important introductions.

I take very good care of my existing clients. I make sure they know how much I appreciate their business and how much I enjoy working with them. I send promotional mailings every six months with samples of recent work. I keep clients updated on awards their projects have received, and I give them transparencies when I shoot them for my portfolio and speaking engagements. My annual marketing budget is about $5,500, including thank you notes, lunches, dinners and gifts. I can't say how many clients have come from these efforts, but I have been able to do some terrific work with top clients and am more profitable than ever."

Although Vrontikis insists that there is no present marketing plan, I think this designer is instinctively doing everything right.

Credit: A.D. Petrula Vrontikis

Innovatively-packaged gift tag collections are given each year to clients and friends of Vrontikis Design Office. "I print the gift tags on the extra room found on press sheets from jobs throughout the year, then in September I design a festive container. This same idea was sold, with matching wrapping paper, to a client for their own promotion." Shown here and on the preceding pages, the last four years' series.

ACCOUNT MANAGEMENT SKILLS:
Keeping the Client

Creating a successful client relationship is based on the same values as any other relationship: honesty, loyalty and trust. Sometimes you are too focused on being The Designer and lose sight of the fact that it is equally important to think about The Business. The best client/designer partnerships occur when you take the time to establish a mutual bond and develop a genuine rapport. This should begin when you are hired for the first project and is ongoing from that point. The same energy that went into "selling" the prospect should be applied to keeping the client. Every day "your" client receives telephone calls, letters and promotional materials from your competition, so never take the relationship for granted, or assume that because you have the job you will continue to keep the client.

After I completed a recent client survey for a fledgling design office, the designer said that the survey information that he found most useful was the emphasis his clients placed on project management. He had been so preoccupied by the problems of the getting the job done on schedule, that he had forgotten how much a client needs to be involved and reassured (sold) as the project goes along. This is especially true with a client you have never worked with before. You are, to quote the title of Harry Beckwith's smart little book, *Selling The Invisible*. From the moment your firm is hired, throughout the creative development and final production phases, confidence in your management ability needs to be constantly reinforced, he stresses. Some clients are more experienced and knowledgeable about the design and production process than others, but they all want, and deserve, the same level of service and accessibility. All are rightly concerned about clear communication, follow-through and good project management. It is revealing how seldom "creativity" and "talent" are mentioned when clients rate design firms. Once you have been hired, creativity is a given and from then on, service is the prevailing issue.

Think of your own experiences as a client and consumer. What makes you loyal to one special store or vendor? If price is not a factor, what drives your decision to chose one among many? Chances are you associate a pleasant personality or positive, cooperative attitude with your final choice. Service is about treating people as though their business matters. Great service involves doing more than what the client expects. Appreciation is one act of civility that often seems to be overlooked in our technology-driven, automated society, so it is especially appreciated when you show that you value your clients' business.

Once you have been hired, creativity is a given and from then on, service is the prevailing issue.

ATTITUDE ADJUSTMENT: YOUR STAFF

Although you as the head of the office, of any size, may have done everything right in winning the confidence of the client, eventually you must delegate some client contact to someone on your staff. This is frequently where all your efforts to develop a good working relationship can collapse. Everyone on your staff should be trained in account management, with emphasis on courtesy, friendliness and dependability. A junior designer is seldom aware of how hard you work to get new business or of how important it is to keep a client happy, and might regard the client as The Enemy of Great Design. The art director's priorities are obviously associated with managing the creative aspect of the project, but he should also take the client relationship into consideration. The receptionist should be told how influential her role in the office actually is. Her voice and her attitude are a direct reflection on you. The office staff represents your company, and the way they deal with a client on the phone and the impression they create when the client personally visits the office are critical to your business.

At the outset of the project the client should be introduced to the people on your staff who will be involved with the job, including the receptionist. She should immediately recognize his name when he calls. Telephone messages, faxes and packages should be logged and delivered immediately; the next day is not good enough. Don't put a staff member in the position of deciding if the message is really important. If a client calls the office and is brusquely "put on hold" or immediately given a recorded voice, he feels unimportant and unwelcome. Although I have to accept the efficiency of the latest telephone technology, it is possible to create a civil, human message even within a mechanized system. Most all recorded voice messages are the same. Wouldn't it make your firm outstanding if you had a better one? Excellent service includes paying attention to many small, often invisible details to make a friendly, cooperative office environment.

REWARD YOUR TEAM

It is wise to share your success with the staff. When the presentation that they worked so hard on is a big hit, tell them. A small celebration, like a mid-afternoon ice cream break or a glass of wine at closing time to mark a special new account acknowledges their contribution to your organization. These little gestures make a big difference in the morale and attitude of the office, resulting in lower staff turnover and a definite quality-of-life bonus. The concept of good service should be a prevailing internal attitude expressed by everyone in the office, from the receptionist to the principal. It's a matter of mutual respect. If the staff is treated as though their contribution to the efficiency and morale of the office is important, they will be more likely to treat others, including clients, accordingly.

SMART HIRING PRACTICES

The April 1998 issue of *Graphic Design/USA* published the results of a survey of key design firms and provided insightful advice, including "The Four Principles of Smart Hiring," which I have adapted as follows:

1. Hire for attitude; train for skill.

Even the best designers won't succeed in your company if they don't fit into the "office culture" with a compatible attitude and character.

2. Know what you're looking for.

The best way to find the personality types you are looking for is to observe the best people already working for you. Find others who, during the interview process, show they can immediately relate to the existing team.

3. The best way to evaluate people is to watch them work.

Consider internship or project-to-permanent assignments as a way to discover how these people fit. This method of hiring has proved to be an excellent way of discovering and retaining top talent.

4. You can't hire people who don't apply.

A high profile as a participating speaker or writer, in addition to having great work published, will attract the best and brightest young people to your firm. Building your reputation is an excellent recruiting strategy.

The survey also points out that burnout and boredom are the main reasons for employees moving on. Design firms have to "be creative, alert and responsive to employees' needs in order to keep the talent they worked so long and hard to find."

GOOD CLIENTS

Clients describe their good relationships with design firms in simple terms: "I like them, they understand us," or "I'm just comfortable working with this design firm, they make it easy for me." Many clients are sophisticated buyers of creative services. Often coming from advertising or marketing backgrounds themselves, they ask practical questions and are not intimidated by the design process. The stereotype of the client as being totally ignorant about design is outdated and untrue. Actually "The Client" is frequently not one individual, but a team of three to twelve people on the decision-making side. Remember too that the client is not the end-user or ultimate customer. Today there is more high-quality graphic design and proportionately more good designers and clients. To be successful, designers must learn what drives the client's needs and become involved in the strategic planning process.

Researching a recent article for *I.D.* magazine, I sent the following questions to a group of clients and designers to discover what their priorities were in selecting and working with each other. A shorter version of the internal and external audit questionnaires, these answers revealed some acute perceptions.

CLIENT/DESIGNER QUESTIONNAIRE

What three things do you look for when hiring a
 design firm?
What is the most important factor in a working relationship?
How much does price affect your selection decision?
Do design awards affect your impression of a firm? How?

Designer/Client Criteria

What are the three most important qualities of a good client?
Can a "bad" client be made into a good one?
What is the biggest problem in client communications?

SOME CLIENT COMMENTS

"A good client is not born. It takes experience and maturity. I don't want to be looked at as The Client. I don't want to be 'serviced.' I want camaraderie and I like to work with designers who help solve problems with me as partners. The firms I hire have mutual interests and are willing to share the risks and rewards of the project."

Bob Ruttenberg, President, Gryphon Development

"We have our own corporate design philosophy and look for a good fit. It's not just a matter of the portfolio, it's a talking and communicating relationship, because the client trusts the designer with a lot of sensitive information."

Leah Caplan, Marketing Director, Filasport

"I look for talented people who understand our issues and are willing to hook up to an established system. In our fast-paced environment, designers have to work quickly. I rely on their fresh perspective to help us continue the program and make it simple."

Kathy Sharpless, Director of Marketing Communications, Putnam Investments

SOME DESIGNER COMMENTS

"Our product is Imagination, but even the most beautiful, hardworking idea has to connect with the needs of the client's business. A good client talks at the beginning and listens in the end. A bad client listens in the beginning and talks in the end. The communication process begins with words."

Susan Slover, Slover & Company

"We look for clients who understand solutions and the meaning of creative thinking. A good client situation is one of a good match. If clients already have a concept, it would be a mismatch to hire a primarily conceptual designer. The best client for us is looking for the least pat solution. Smarter clients look deeper, their level of involvement is directly related to their level of experience and they know what design can do. The client and designer are on the same, not opposing, sides. The issue is not who gets the credit. For us, the real ego satisfaction comes out of a successful project."

Curt Altmann, Partner, Storm Design

"A client can be incredibly demanding and still be a great client. We will knock ourselves out to please him because we know he really cares. We may not always agree, but we have a mutual objective. The failure of a client relationship is due to either false expectations or poor communications. Conservative clients have preconceived ideas and expect the conventional use of imagery, but we want to be challenged, to go beyond the expected. Good design can accomplish exceptional results."

Michael McGinn, Principal, Designframe

PROJECT MANAGEMENT: CREATING A SYSTEM

Initially you will be hired for your creative ability and experience, but once the client has made a commitment, you must continue to deliver on your original promise. A project can take many months before it is finally produced, and there will be many frustrating delays, miscommunications, rewrites and revisions during this period. Your job, in addition to providing the best design solution, is to keep the project on track and the client involved and regularly informed. Every office needs to develop a management system that allows it to effectively act and interact with the client side.

Although this book is primarily focused on new business development and account management, the following discussion of legal contracts and forms is addressed because it is critical to the ultimate success of your company. Every aspect of the business should be conducted on the highest ethical and professional level, and all correspondence, including proposals and contracts, should be typo-free and absolutely accurate. Not only does this discipline and attention to detail prevent future misunderstandings, or worse, but it establishes you to clients and vendors as an intelligent businessperson.

Every office needs to develop a management system that allows it to effectively act and interact with the client side.

CONTRACT QUESTIONS

Every contract should answer these questions

1. What does the designer offer/promise to do?
Description of Project, Schedule

2. What will it cost?
Schedule of Payment, including % of fee in advance

3. What are the terms and conditions?
Delivery Date, Expenses, Changes, Cancellation,
Usage Rights

4. What are the obligations of the client?
Respect delivery schedule by providing copy in a
timely manner, sign and return change orders,
payment as agreed.

The AIGA (American Institute of Graphic Arts) has developed for its members a Standard Form of Agreement for Graphic Design Services that has served as the contract benchmark for the past ten years. The AIGA contract form is probably much more extensive than you need for an average job, so I also recommend the simpler agreement forms found in *Business and Legal Forms for Graphic Designers* by Tad Crawford and Eva Doman Bruck, published by Allworth Press. It offers a complete overview of this subject including ready-to-use forms. These and the *Graphic Artists Guild Handbook, Pricing and Ethical Guidelines* should be within reach of your desk for reference. You do not have to reinvent the wheel. Originality does not count here, so be grateful for these wise resources and use them.

THE PAPER TRAIL

The paper trail usually begins with the Proposal/ Letter of Agreement, a clear description of the job, estimated fees, schedule of payment, delivery date, if possible, and terms and conditions. Although this serves as a binding contract, most design firms do not like the term "contract," preferring instead to use this less intimidating form.

The Letter of Agreement proposal format is constructed to include the basic job description and terms describing what you will do, how long it will take and what it will cost. This information allows the client to compare competitive quotes. You should be clear about the client's responsibilities such as providing copy, proofreading and approval of final artwork. It should not be assumed that the client always understands that photography, illustrations, printing, reimbursable expenses and sales tax are not included here. This agreement is strictly dealing with "design services." The form should always be signed and dated by you and the client.

Remember that this is still a preliminary estimate of the job, so don't be too specific about the terms of the job such as the delivery schedule or estimated charges if you do not have all of the information at this early stage. If this estimate is agreed to, a final, more detailed set of terms can be covered in a following letter.

Even in the simplest Letter of Agreement form, the following statement should appear: "This proposal will serve as our agreement. Please sign and date in the space below, and return one copy."

Here is an example of a typical Proposal form. Rather than creating a new document for each prospective project, it saves time, and discourages client changes, when you print your own Standard Proposal Form:

PROPOSAL

Client name   Date

Title   Delivery by

Company

Address

Project

Project Description

Phase I   Schedule   Fee

Conceptual Planning

and Research

Phase II   Schedule   Fee

Creative Development

and Design

Phase III   Schedule   Fee

Implementation/Production

Schedule of Payment:

Terms:

Client Signature   **Designer Signature**

Company   Date

Designating a chain of command, those who will be responsible for approval and signing off on changes, should be established at the outset. Change Order Forms are essential, particularly on bigger jobs, and a Weekly Update is a good way to provide information about the progress of the project. Every designer has a few war stories of jobs that went very wrong. Usually the fault can be traced to misunderstandings and poorly communicated responsibilities.

The ability to compromise and cooperate will keep a job moving ahead, you should see yourself as working "with" a client, not working "for" him. There has to be a lead vision that becomes the mutual goal of both parties. If the concept or execution is not right, a client should feel free to say so, and the designer must be able to accept it as a professional, not a personal, critique.

The most successful design firms have the additional ability of making people feel comfortable. This is not only a characteristic of good salesmanship, but one of empathy. Selling is an emotional, not an intellectual activity. Understanding that the corporate way of communicating is frequently non-confrontational and generalized, a designer must be able to draw the client into an open dialogue to express at the beginning of the project what he needs and where the problems are. And when the job is finished, it is vital to follow up by meeting with the client to analyze the job and discuss where project management improvements are needed. Constructive suggestions and criticism should be welcome, and clients appreciate this opportunity to express their thoughts. An internal staff debriefing is equally important not only for pointing out weaknesses but to praise and reinforce good performance. Deal with any problems at this point, before risking the loss of dissatisfied clients. Clear the air, and move on.

The ability to compromise and cooperate will keep a job moving ahead, you should see yourself as working "with" a client, not working "for" him.

AFTERMARKETING AND CROSS-SELLING

Aftermarketing, including follow-up meetings, is an aspect of marketing that is often overlooked. Going after a fresh target seems more challenging, but the fact is most of your business will be repeat business. Take care to cultivate the good clients you have; they are your future.

Cross-selling refers to taking advantage of often-missed opportunities. Once you have worked with a company you are no longer an outsider, but a valuable resource. Since you now have an understanding of the industry and the goals of your client, you should be looking for additional related projects within the company. If you have designed the annual report yours should be considered the most obvious firm to design collateral marketing literature, the CD-ROM or video version of the report. Designers frequently think only short term, working from one project to another without selling themselves as a long-term design partner.

REFERRALS

How can you encourage referrals? First, by doing good work: innovative design that satisfies the client and makes you proud. Not only do you want to continue to work with them on bigger and better projects, you want them to recommend your firm to their peers. While the glow following a successful job is still warm, ask the client for a referral letter. He will usually be happy to comply. These referrals are precious. Many established firms rely almost entirely on referrals for new business. Think of how much time and effort is saved when a prospect comes to you, pre-sold, eager to meet you and see your work, pure gold. The referral/testimonial letter can be included in future proposal packages and is invaluable in reinforcing your reputation and credibility.

There is nothing like the praise of a satisfied client so use this referral letter whenever appropriate. And it is considered good form to first ask the client for permission to use his letter as part of your marketing program.

FIRING BAD CLIENTS

Considering how hard it is to get clients, you may be surprised to learn that occasionally you will need to fire one. In the beginning of your design practice you will most likely charge clients less than what you think you deserve. You may feel obliged to take a job with a person that you frankly don't like, or a company that is not a good fit with your future design specialization. Life is too short to work for people who make you feel undervalued. You cannot do your best work under stressful, unpleasant conditions, and as much as you believe that it is unprofessional not to be able to work with every kind of client, the fact is, you don't have to. If a client is not willing to pay you higher fees as your business grows, then you have a choice between working for less than what you are charging new accounts, or getting rid of the old client. Some sentimental souls continue to work with those original clients, but if they respect you and value your work they will pay the new rate, even if reluctantly. Selecting who you want to develop a long-term working relationship with is an empowering feeling. Firing a client is painful but necessary in order to make room for the people who are fun to work with and willing to pay you fairly for your services.

Life is too short to work for people who make you feel undervalued.

ART AND COMPROMISE

Much of what you learned on the school playground about sharing and generally getting along with everyone applies to your professional conduct. For the artist, however, compromise is an extremely sensitive issue. The process of arriving at what you consider to be the best design solution is a long and thoughtful one, and when a client rejects your work it feels like a personal insult. You bought into your own solution, but now you can't sell it to the client. What should you do? Having spent a dozen years as a designer, I well understand the feelings of stubbornness and hurt when your work is rejected. I applaud the designer who can easily pick himself up and start working on a new solution, and this is what you must train yourself to do. As hard as it may be to accept criticism, I don't believe that there is only one good idea or a single right solution to a problem.

If you have taped or taken good notes at that last meeting, the client has probably raised some valid points and made a few constructive suggestions. Review client objections away from the conference room and analyze whether these criticisms are accurate. Try to look at it from the other side. What are the needs of the client? If the type is too small for him to read easily, then it is probably too small for the shareholders he is mailing this annual report to. The recent tiny-type fashion did not make a lot of friends outside of the design world. Be open to constructive criticism, don't be arrogant. But if the client has no good reason why he hates your choice of color other than the fact that his favorite color is green, perhaps there is some shade of green that will please both of you and the integrity of the design concept will not suffer. Be flexible. You have been hired to solve the client's communication design problem, not to express your own creativity. An emotional temper tantrum is exactly the reaction businesspeople expect from designers, so be unpredictably mature.

NEGOTIATING

What is negotiation? In his book, *How To Negotiate Anything*, Herb Cohen describes negotiation as "a field of knowledge and endeavor focused on gaining the favor of people from whom we want things." Generally speaking, negotiation is the use of information and power to affect behavior. We do this every day, in dealing with our partners, our employees, our clients and our vendors, hopefully reaching a conclusion where both parties leave feeling that they have won their objectives. Negotiation is not an exercise in proving strength but in demonstrating intelligence and sensitivity.

Usually negotiation problems revolve around services and money. Even within the best relationships, misunderstandings can occur. This is the primary reason for creating a written agreement at the outset of a project.

In the education of a designer, compromise and negotiation are subjects given little attention. It is only when a designer finds himself across the conference table from his client with a contract between them that he discovers the gap in his professional preparation. School is all about originality and self-expression; business is negotiation and teamwork. This is one of the main reasons why you want to chose your clients carefully. If there is that "good fit" and you have a mutual respect and understanding, negotiation is a reasonable exchange between equals. Without a solid foundation of respect, negotiation about money or design can be an exercise in humiliation and defeat. It doesn't have to be.

TROUBLESHOOTING: TEN IMPORTANT TIPS

Before, during and after a job you should remember to review the following points:

1. Never Assume. Put it in Writing

Put everything in writing. Get written approvals for changes, extra charges, and soon. In the original contract, describe fees, responsibilities and delivery of the project. Nothing is obvious to everyone. Keep a daily log of the job, noting problems, and send a weekly update to the client.

2. Everything is Negotiable

Anticipate negotiations; be flexible. Don't be intimidated, but be prepared to bend when necessary. See where costs can be cut without impairing the integrity of the design or goals of the client.

3. Watch the Clock. Time is Money

In a service business you are selling your time. It is not unlimited. Learn to wisely manage the number of hours spent on the project by you or your staff. Treat the client's money as though it were your own. Respect the client's time. This job is not the only thing on his agenda.

4. Pay Attention to Details: Small Stuff Counts

From the earliest contact, pay attention to things like getting names spelled correctly and proper titles in letters. Remember the secretary's name. Return phone calls, faxes and E-mail messages promptly.

5. Scheduling: Don't Promise What You Can't Deliver

Are you creating your own failure by offering the impossible? Don't promise a service or price that is unreasonable or beyond your experience. It is better to have to ask for an extension than fail to deliver as promised. You will not get a second chance.

6. The Killer Deadline: Do Whatever it Takes

Make every effort to to complete the job in a professional, timely manner. Don't lose your focus, your control or your temper. Put in as many late hours as the work requires and do whatever it takes.

7. Following Up: Post-Mortem

Learn from your experiences, good as well as bad. What makes a job a success or a failure? Don't wait until the project is over; address problems as soon as possible. After the job is finished meet with the client, staff and possibly vendors, to discuss the project and how it could have been improved. Even if it was perfect, show why. You will reinforce your competence in project management, and validate the client's original decision to hire you. This is advance selling.

8. Reward Yourself. Reward Your Staff

Promise yourself a reward when the job is over—a box of Belgian chocolates, a trip to Paris, a new surfboard—whatever you need to get you through that occasional job-from-hell. Acknowledge your own good performance as well as that of your employees. They deserve more than their paychecks for work above and beyond the call of duty—a few days off, a performance bonus, maybe a gift certificate at their favorite shop. Celebrate all work well done.

9. Be a Professional: Don't Take it Personally

In every aspect of your work—internal office operations, and personnel, vendor and client relationships—situations will test your patience and experience. Always be professional. Try to remain rational and objective. Don't let emotions make you say something you will later regret. Count to ten, breathe deeply, it's just business.

10. Build a Support System: Ask for Help

It is absolutely critical to build a network of experts whom you can count on for professional advice and technical information; technicians in all computer and office equipment-related services, printing and paper salespeople, an accountant and a good business lawyer. Have lunch with some fellow designers whom you admire and develop a colleague relationship. As a student or young designer, you may be fortunate enough to find a mentor. If you have a more established practice, consider becoming a mentor yourself. Be curious. Ask questions. Don't wait for an emergency before you look for help.

CHAPTER **10**

CONTINUING EDUCATION:
The Thinking Designer

IMPROVING PROFESSIONAL PERFORMANCE

Even with the best design education and a thriving practice, smart designers know they must continually update and expand their professional knowledge. What does this have to do with marketing? Just as you seek the best and latest hardware and software to equip your office, learning new business skills gives your firm a competitive edge and prepares you for the more complex design practice of the future.

Lately business gurus have co-opted the word that once was the exclusive property of designers and artists: Creativity. Tom

Peters, in his book, *The Pursuit of WOW*, says, "Business, in the mad global marketplace, needs a rush of serious creativity." Conversely, I think that creative professionals need a serious rush of business. A designer's creativity is primarily a visual experience. By nature and a rather narrow education, designers express themselves in terms of color, form and line. Business creativity is a matter of effecting changes in behavior. Instead of making something beautiful, the focus is on producing value and results. Understanding each other's methods and rationale allow designers and clients to collaborate on mutually successful work.

BACK TO SCHOOL: MASTERS DEGREE PROGRAMS IN DESIGN MANAGEMENT

How can a busy designer continue his education and learn to play a strategic role in more diverse and profitable projects?

Pratt Institute, New York

I recently met with Robert Anders, Program Head of the Design Management Program at Pratt Institute in New York, to discuss their unique program.

I think that creative professionals need a serious rush of business.

"We offer a two-year, weekend class schedule leading to the academic degree of Master of Professional Studies (M.P.S.) in Design Management. Modeled after successful executive M.B.A. programs throughout the country, our program allows participants to carry their full-time job responsibilities while they study. This is the first and only program like this in the United States, created for practicing designers including industrial designers, architects, interior designers, fashion designers, graphic designers and others who want to be more." Courses include Strategic Marketing, Advertising and Promotion, Leadership and Team-Building, Negotiating, Business Law, Managerial Decision-Making and Business Planning.

Why do you think a designer needs this additional education experience?

"Designers are not trained in the language; of business, they have their own priorities, their own language. The Design Management Program teaches how to join the business team as an equal player, sharing a common language. Designers can then enter the business environment with the ability to communicate with business-educated leaders."

What classes do you think are the most important?

"Every class is built on something else. They cannot be separated. There are six spheres of knowledge not previously covered in a designer's education: people, money, management, marketing, law and business history, and strategy and analysis. Each element is critical."

What books are required student reading?
Recommended Reading List Includes:

Schultz, Don E. Tannenbaum, Stanley I.,
and Anne Allison
Essentials of Advertising Strategy, 3rd ed.
NTC Business Books, 1995.

Drucker, Peter F.
Managing for the Future: The 1990's and Beyond.
New York: Truman Talley Books/Dutton, 1992.

Funk, Jeffrey L.
The Teamwork Advantage.
Cambridge: Productivity Press, 1992.

Gates, Bill
The Road Ahead.
New York: Penguin Books, 1996.

Kao, John.
Jamming: The Art and Discipline of Business Creativity.
New York: Harper Collins, 1996.

Kennedy, Paul.
Preparing for the Twenty-First Century.
New York: Random House, 1993.

McRae, Hamish.
The World in 2020: Power, Culture and Prosperity.
Boston: Harvard Business School Press, 1994.

Naisbitt, John.
Global Paradox.
New York: William Morrow and Company, Inc. 1994.

Peters, Tom.
*The Tom Peters Seminar: Crazy Times Call For
Crazy Organizations.*
New York: Vintage Books, 1994.

Peters, Tom.
The Pursuit of WOW
New York: Random House, 1994.

Toffler, Alvin.
*Power Shift: Knowledge, Wealth and Violence at the
Edge of the 21st Century.*
New York: Bantam Books, 1990.

**What are your thoughts on the future of the design
profession?**

"I am very optimistic about the future for designers. The business world recognizes that design is the only way to distinguish one product from another, and that good design directly contributes to the bottom line. As the media grows to include more communication vehicles than ever before—cable, Internet, Web sites, etc.—more intelligent designers are needed. The design profession is maturing and gaining authority and there are many new opportunities for those who can speak both the language of design and business."

Anders told me that one-third to one-half of the students in his program are from in-house corporate design departments. For a designer with your own practice, learning these new skills will give you access to immediately usable information. Not only will you have additional tools to work with in your business relationships, this knowledge provides you greater confidence and range.

WHAT PRATT GRADUATES AND STUDENTS SAY

"The program was a deep learning experience that went beyond facts, figures and definitions. Every day I use class-learned techniques in strategic planning, production management, negotiation, consensus-building, innovation, quality control and team-building. I credit the program with my position and success as the design manager of The New York Botanical Garden. I now have the confidence to begin consulting in design as well as writing, marketing and strategic planning. The graduate program has profoundly affected the way I think about design and ultimately helped me to develop lifetime goals."
Maria Ruotolo
Design Management and Planning Consultant

"Halfway through the graduate program, upper management was impressed by my combination of design and business skills and promoted me from product designer to design manager of the private brand housewares development department. Today I am managing four full-time designers and a large group of freelancers. Developing products with manufacturing facilities in Asia and Europe convinced me that challenges in the design field are on a global scale. Companies need designers who can build vision and strategy, present concepts, negotiate with manufacturers or services, and promote the talents of the staff. I am now better equipped to understand business concerns and run an effective department to meet the needs of demanding consumers."

James Murray, Design Manager
Federated Merchandising Group
(a division of Federated Department Stores)

"After thinking about it for ten years, I decided to go back to graduate school. In order to have a competitive advantage in today's market I needed an informational balance between my creative side and the business world. There is no power in this field like the power of knowledge. Designers should never underestimate the amount of business information they need to be successful. This program has given me new confidence, motivation and understanding. Creative empowerment comes when you understand how the other side works."

Sarah J. Hall
SJH Design + Studio

My advice to prospective students . . . Do it!
AnneLouise Burns

"I've worked for myself for a number of years, and wanted to learn how to run my business more effectively. The Design Management Program actually made me want to go back to school because it is geared to the specific business and working conditions of designers. My advice to prospective students . . . Do it! Be prepared for lots of hard, self-revealing, inspirational, exhilarating and rewarding work. It is amazing how much you will learn. Some of the most valuable classes were Leadership and Teambuilding, Marketing Professional Services and Business Information Sources. The friendships that developed within the class are ongoing. Because we all have the same "tool kit" and shared experience, we seek each other out to brainstorm and discuss particular problems; it's a unique and wonderful connection."

AnneLouise Burns
Blue Sky Design Company

FULL-TIME MASTERS DEGREE PROGRAMS

In Chicago, The Institute of Design (ID) at Illinois Institute of Technology provides a unique, full-time, graduate school that offers a Masters of Design (M.Des.) degree as well as the nation's only Ph.D. in design. The Masters program has four areas of specialization: strategic design planning, communication design, product design, and photography. Students with prior experience complete the program in two years.

John Heskett has been a professor of design theory at ID since 1989. His work is concerned with design as a policy instrument in governments and corporations, and the economic relationships between design and innovation.

"We teach a basic methodology to equip our graduates with the capability of functioning at the strategic planning level, integrating design into the whole picture. In the first year, we have an intensive program to equip students with the necessary concepts and competencies. In the second year, students focus on a major project, like a thesis, to demonstrate their command of what has been taught. The average age of our students is 29, so most of them have had nine or ten years of work experience. Of the thousands of art school graduates every year, the shocking fact is that only 7-12% of them will get jobs in the field. In contrast, all of our students get good jobs. Our program, which deals with understanding major factors in business organizations' market strategy, operations and innovation, assures that the design professional is prepared to create usable, human-centered solutions"

INTERVIEWS: ID GRADUATES

I spoke with two graduates of the Institute of Design program; Jim Ludwigs was trained as a chemical engineer and spent 12 years working on process and chip design for Intel before deciding to go into ID's Graduate Program. "It was not that I was dissatisfied with my job, but I thought that while I was young enough, I wanted to acquire new and unique business skills. It took me three and a half years to make the decision to leave the security of my job, and another two and a half to get though the program. I am now responsible for new service and new business development at Ernst and Young, an international consulting group in New York. I love it." I asked Jim what were his most valuable classes and their benefits. "I found the best classes emphasized structure and planning. John Heskett's courses teach the design management position relative to other disciplines, and they connect with real-world experience. ID's program has a way of catching up with you; you're not sure of its value until you get out." Observing designers at ID, Jim remarked, "They generally lack the ability to talk about their processes, as though intuition doesn't really need to be inspected. The benefit of the program is that it gives you a vocabulary in a business-based context, and teaches the value of process. Designers tend to run away from structure. My tip, get all the information about structure you can. The distance I have traveled has been enormous, it has really paid off. "

Christine Costello comes from a fine arts background and worked as a graphic designer for six years before she decided to move on. She saw that the computer would change not only the daily life of the designer, but also what design was about. "I recognized that a split had occurred in the design world between product and strategy, and I needed to restructure how I could think through a project. Aesthetic problem-solving was not helping me. I wanted to learn business-based issues, methods and processes. The ID program was a great fit for me because it integrated the skills I already had with new strategies, it gave me a great mental toolbox. I couldn't believe how powerful behavior analysis research could be. Few design people are taught the value of strategic planning, but how can you think about design if you don't also consider the user's technology and business strategy? There is no comparison between my previous work and the level of work I do now. I've turned into a different kind of designer by learn-

The benefit of the program is that it gives you a vocabulary in a business-based context, and teaches the value of process.
Jim Ludwigs

ing to understand technology, social effects, and how to think from a user perspective. Personally and professionally, going back to school is one of the best things I've ever done."

Costello is now a Corporate and Product Design Leader for Art Technology Group in Boston, a company that designs and develops new media products and services sold over the Internet.

Designers who return to school after years of experience in the field recognize that they need more tools in order to advance their careers. The value of this advanced education to the already established designer is seen in the more comprehensive range of capabilities they develop. High-level employment opportunities have opened up in major corporations, design, and management consultancies. For the graduates of a Masters program, the reward is expressed by a generous starting salary, often comparable to those offered to M.B.A. graduates. I am very impressed with these programs and would not hesitate to recommend graduate school for any designer who discovers that he or she has a head for business and a desire to focus on broader issues than those strictly concerned with design.

Personally and professionally, going back to school is one of the best things I've ever done.

Christine Costello

EXTENSION PROGRAM COURSES

If you do not have the time or inclination to pursue a full- or part-time Masters degree program, there are many available courses in advertising, marketing, leadership and management offered at local schools and universities as part of their extension programs. It is not necessary for the course to be specifically created for design professionals. For example, an advertising course will cover strategies, market targeting, and promotion; it may also include copy-writing. Learning to think beyond the usual two-dimensional concerns provides you with richer experience and perspective, and makes you a key player in the client's project from the early planning stages.

Parsons School of Design Continuing Education in New York City offers a variety of classes which teach important design concepts and skills. Pamela Vassil, who heads this program says that the designers who will succeed are the ones who "can talk the talk" as well as design. She stresses language skills and insists that writing courses are equally relevant to computer ones. "Graphic design services The Word. The two are inseparable, otherwise design is merely surface decoration. Today, the trend is not about reading (literacy), but at the very core of good design is an understanding of what you are designing for, the concept. The best designers . . . read."

Although the class may include material outside of what you consider to be your immediate needs, every business-based subject will contribute to an understanding of this new language, just as your knowledge of a foreign language on any level improves your ability to communicate. It is up to you whether your goal is to just cover the basics, or advancing to the level of expressing yourself with total fluency. Speaking literally of foreign languages, with technologies that allow us to communicate with the world with previously unimagined ease, the knowledge of another language could be helpful in working with countries in Europe, Latin America and Asia, so if you have a gift for languages, why not consider studying one that may be appropriate in your prospective market.

PLAYING THE GAME OF BUSINESS

At the very core of good design is an understanding of what you are designing for, the concept. The best designers read.

Pamela Vassil

In Chapter Two I recommended a sample list of books and audio tapes on sales, marketing and negotiating. The purpose of this information, within the context of the the marketing or account persons' role, is to provide motivation and a pragmatic knowledge of subjects needed to increase sales. While this kind of material is certainly important, your education has to go deeper if you are to make a more profound change in your understanding of the business mentality. It requires an important shift in attitude from the solo artist to team player or leader. The game of business can be elegant as well as intelligent, and team strategy is an equally creative contribution to the total solution.

Much of what you need to learn now is how to lose certain elitist attitudes about The Business World vs. The Design World, because as soon as you established your own office, you became part of that other side of life. Understanding money, marketing principles and how to work effectively with people will give you a new sense of empowerment, and by employing well-conceived strategy and analysis skills in the developmental phases of the work, your level of professionalism is raised to a higher, more respected level than if you simply worked from an intuitive, instinctive sense of design. Keep in mind that, in most cases, your continuing education expenses are tax-deductible. Check with your accountant.

EDUCATIONAL BENEFITS

Not only should you seek relevant business courses for your own continuing education, you should encourage your employees to enroll in these courses as well. Paying for this ongoing education is a much-appreciated employee benefit. Often a class in marketing, copy-writing or presentation skills for a few of the staff raises the level of quality and standards for the entire office.

If classes are not available in your area, build a good library of books, videos and audio tapes and encourage frequent use. Consider the graduate degree distance learning courses offered by many universities on-line. Hire a consultant to give Saturday or evening seminars in the office in any business-based subject you and the staff are interested in. Not only should you advance your own education, it's a good management strategy to share the experience and allow your staff to grow with you. Your clients and vendors are also a great, untapped resource for information and expertise. Consider including them in one of your Saturday or evening panel discussions, seminars or workshops as participants or speakers. There are considerable advantages in taking the responsibility for these sessions, not the least of which is the fact that they are hosted by your office, on your own turf . . . "the home-court advantage."

Here are a few suggested topics;

1. What Makes a Successful Identity Program?
2. How to Create a Memorable Advertising Campaign
3. Get the Most from Your Printing & Paper Budgets
4. The Best Marketing Strategies: Case Studies
5. The Annual Report Workshop
6. International Packaging Trends and Technology
7. Roundtable Discussion: Improving our Environment through Design
8. How to Get Maximum Performance from Your Interactive Communications
9. Advanced Leadership and Team-Building Skills
10. Successful Project Management: What Do Clients Want Most?

BECOMING AN ACTIVE MEMBER

Find local chapters of organizations that interest you and attend a few meetings to see if you might fit into their program as a participating member or speaker; for example, the Chamber of Commerce, The Rotary Club, or sales and marketing associations. Don't join an organization unless you are ready to take an active part in it. Passing your business card around at a monthly luncheon is not "active." Become a member of a committee, or volunteer for an event. Offer to redesign their newsletter or logo, if this would be welcome.

READ, READ, READ

Read, and keep reading everything you can to keep you informed about your city, state, country, planet. Regular reading of The Wall Street Journal, Newsweek, Forbes, Inc.,Fast Company and other business and news publications will familiarize you with current issues that are of importance to your clients. Eventually you will share these concerns and language. Become comfortable in the non-designer world.

BUILDING YOUR OWN TEAM: PARTNERING

Your personal and professional growth should extend beyond your own individual capabilities, and as your practice matures, it's obvious that your core staff cannot perform every creative and technical service. Sometimes you may need to collaborate with outsiders as joint project partners. Building a team requires that you have the ability to recognize talents in others. Hire people who are not like you. Don't look for clones or people who follow directions slavishly, look for people who challenge and stimulate you and the rest of the team. This principle should include not only full-time staff members but freelancers and consultants. Make connections with people who will not only bring their special talents to the job, but also intelligence, energy and passion. Establish a network of collaborators—architects, public relations and advertising agencies, photographers, illustrators, writers, industrial and environmental designers, computer geniuses, etc. Always be searching for the best in his or her field and spend time meeting with them personally. Building these strategic alliances allows you to have the ability to put together the best creative team for a particular project. It is well worth developing these relationships in advance of your needs because personal chemistry and trust take time. There is also the likelihood that they will be pleased to reciprocate by recommending your firm. Smart people know how necessary it is to work with other smart people, and value those they have the privilege to know.

Building a team requires that you have the ability to recognize talents in others. Hire people who are not like you.

ESTABLISHING AN INTERNSHIP PROGRAM

Be inclusive, not exclusive. Establish an internship program with a nearby college or university with a design or marketing program. This usually means giving a student the opportunity to work in your office as a paid or unpaid intern whose duties will be mostly in an entry-level or pre-entry level capacity (a lot of go fer work). The eager young intern can relieve your staff from mundane chores like filing, stuffing, labeling, and trips to the post office or stationery supply store. In return, you offer him or her a chance to observe the day-to-day functioning of a professional design firm. This real-life experience is priceless for a student, and often it gives the design firm a chance to train someone who will later become part of the staff after graduation.

MARKETING YOUR NEW CAPABILITIES

Hoping that you have taken my advice and expanded your office's capabilities through a series of accelerated educational efforts and new collaborative relationships, you now can offer clients additional consultant services that go well beyond graphic design. Frequently firms with strategic planning, marketing and branding disciplines work with a company on projects that do not include design at all. The experience with and understanding of problems that deeply concern the bottom line of the client makes a designer with planning and organizational abilities an important, integrated partner. No longer satisfied only to create an award-winning design and move on to the next project, the designer who can work on business-based goals will become part of the client's strategic team. Because you are now part of the company's long-range plan, you should feel more secure, but not too secure, about your relationship and be compensated for your thinking as well as your creative talents. Remember that there is no guarantee of loyalty. You must not only continue to deliver on your original promise, you have to surpass it.

The marketing strategy for your firm should now communicate these new capabilities they may provide the edge that wins you the assignment over your competitors. Brochure copy and press releases should highlight these added services and explain the benefits to prospective and existing clients. Case studies are especially good at showing examples of how you have been able to affect a successful outcome, and client testimonials can give credibility to your new capabilities. We never tire of hearing those Cinderella or Before/After stories. Use every positive, interesting message available to sell your firm's range of business-wise abilities.

PROGRAM FOR THE FUTURE

In the past, the growth of a design practice was measured by the size of the staff, quality of the clients and the annual revenues produced. Design firms believed that by continuing to build a profitable client base commensurate with their ability to win awards and recognition, they were operating successfully. Today, and in the future, the design profession will become more complex, more deeply involved in understanding and resolving the business issues of the client. You can no longer rely on your art school education to carry you through your entire professional life.

As we go to press, I have news of an exciting undergraduate course being offered for the first time in the spring of 1999 at North Carolina State University's College of Management and taught by faculty in the Departament of Graphic Design. The Graphic Design and Business Course is available to graphic designers, as well as management students. This rare chance for both disciplines to study together provides an excellent way to develop a basic, mutual understanding between business and design. The objectives of the course, as described are:

1. to introduce students to the strategic opportunities design represents for business and to understand the advantages of placing design at the front end of corporate decisionmaking

2. to prepare students to manage design as one of several integrated business processes

3. to explain and illustrate the design process—to better understand the work of designers and project timelines.

Meridith Davis, professor and director of the Graduate Program is enthusiastic and hopeful about this crucial new development.

"At no time in the history of our discipline has design management been more important to the survival and definition of graphic design than at present."

Designers who want a greater part in the successes of the corporate world must be willing to share in the risks as well. This means that you have to prepare yourself to take an active, participatory role on the client side, learning how to plan marketplace strategies and management realities. Tomorrow will be challenging and profoundly more exciting than you ever imagined back in school. Those designers who are willing to stretch their intuitive talents to include deeper analytical skills will discover rewarding new sources of professional and personal accomplishment.

DESIGN SCHOOLS

ABCD American Business Center of Design
California Polytechnic
University, Pomona
7450 Olivetas Avenue #B9
La Jolla, CA 92037
(619) 450–5379
FAX (619) 450–5298

ACA College of Design
2528 Kemper Lane
Cincinnati, OH 45206
(513) 751–1206
FAX (513) 751–1209

Academy of Art College
79 New Montgomery Street
San Francisco, CA 94105
(415) 274–2247
FAX (415) 546–9737

Arizona State University
School of Design
Box 87210
Tempe, AZ 85287
(602) 965–4135
FAX (602) 965–9717

Art Center College of Design
1700 Lida Street
Pasadena, CA 91103
(818) 396–2200
FAX (818) 405–9104

Art Institute of Boston
700 Beacon Street
Boston, MA 02215
(617) 262–1223
FAX (617) 437–1226

Art Institute of Chicago
37 South Wabash Avenue
Chicago, IL 60603
(312) 899–5100
FAX (312) 263–0141

Art Institute of Seattle
2323 Elliot Avenue
Seattle, WA 98121
(206) 448–6600
FAX (206) 448–2501

Art Institute of Southern California
2222 Laguna Canyon Road
Laguna Beach, CA 92651
(714) 497–3309
FAX (714) 497–4399

Associated Design Service
11160 Southwest Highway
Palos Hills, IL 60465
(708) 974–9100
FAX (708) 974–4975

Auburn University
O.D. Smith Hall
Auburn, AL 36849
(334) 844–2364

Cal State Northridge
Art/3 D Media Department
18111 Nordhoff Street
Northridge, CA 91330
(818) 885–2784
FAX (818) 885–4540

California College
of Arts & Crafts
5212 Broadway
Oakland, CA 94618
(510) 653–8118
FAX (510) 655–3541

California State
at Long Beach
1250 Bellflower Boulevard
Long Beach, CA 90840
(310) 985–5089
FAX (310) 985–2284

California State at Fullerton
Environmental Design/Visual
Arts Center
Fullerton, CA 92634
(714) 773–2075
FAX (714) 773–3005

Carnegie-Mellon University
Design Department
College of Fine Arts
MMCH 110
Pittsburgh, PA 15213
(412) 268–2828
FAX (412) 268–3088

Center for Creative Studies
201 East Kirby Street
Detroit, MI 48202
(313) 872–3118
FAX (313) 872–8377

Center for Electronic Art
250 Fourth Street
San Francisco, CA 94103
(415) 512–9300
FAX (415) 512–9260

Cleveland Institute of Art
11141 East Boulevard
University Circle
Cleveland, OH 44106
(216) 421–7000
FAX (216) 421–7438

College of Visual Arts
344 Summit Avenue
St. Paul, MN 55102
(612) 224–3416
FAX (612) 224–8854

Columbia College
600 South Michigan Avenue
Chicago, IL 60605
(312) 663–1600

Columbus College
of Art & Design
107 North Ninth Street
Columbus, OH 43215
(614) 224–9101
FAX 222–4040

**Connecticut College
Department of Art/Design
Studies**
Center for Art & Technology
270 Mohegan Avenue
New London, CT 06320
(203) 439–2748
FAX (203) 439–5339

**Cooper Union
for the Advancement
of Science & Art**
30 Cooper Square
New York, NY 10003
(212) 353–4200
FAX (212) 353–4345

Cranbrook Academy of Art
Box 801
1221 North Woodward Avenue
Bloomfield Hills, MI 48303
(810) 645–3300
FAX (810) 646–0046

Creative Center
11128 John Galt Boulevard
Omaha, NE 68137
(402) 339–6001
FAX (402) 339–6001

**Desktop Design & Publishing
Training Center Inc.**
45 East Main Street
Freehold, NJ 07728
(908) 409–2635

**Drexel University College
of Design Arts**
Philadelphia, PA 19104
(215) 895–2386
FAX (215) 895–4917

**Fashion Institute
of Technology**
Seventh Avenue at 27th Street
New York, NY 10001
(212) 760–7665
FAX (212) 760–7160

**Georgia Institute
of Technology**
College of Architecture/Industrial
Design Program
Atlanta, GA 30332
(404) 894–4874
FAX (404) 894–3396

**Georgia Institute
of Technology**
Office of Interdisciplinary
Programs
250 14th Street NW #M14
Atlanta, GA 30332
(404) 894–4195
FAX (404) 894–7339

**Illinois Institute of
Technology/Institute
of Design (IIT)**
10 West 35th Street
Chicago, IL 60616
(312) 808–5300
FAX (312) 808–5322

Iowa State University
158 College of Design
Ames, IA 50011
(515) 294–6724
FAX (515) 294–2725

Kansas City Art Institute
4415 Warwick Boulevard
Kansas City, MO 64111
(816) 561–4852
FAX (816) 561–6404

**Kendall College
of Art & Design**
111 Division AVenue North
Grand Rapids, MI 49503
(616) 451–2787
FAX (616) 451–9867

**Kent State University
School of Art**
Kent, OH 44242
(216) 672–2192
FAX (216) 672–4729

Maine College of Art
97 Spring Street
Portland, ME 04101
(207) 775–3052
FAX (207) 772–5069

**Massachusetts College
of Art/Industrial Design**
621 Huntington Avenue
Boston, MA 02115
(617) 232–1555
FAX (617) 566–4034

**Michigan State University
Department of Art**
East Lansing, MI 48824
(517) 355–7638
FAX (517) 432–3938

**Milwaukee Institute
of Art & Design**
273 East Erie Street
Milwaukee, WI 53202
(414) 276–7889
FAX (414) 291–8077

**Moore College
of Art & Design**
The Parkway at 20th Street
Philadelphia, PA 19103
(215) 568–4515
FAX (215) 568–8017

**North Carolina State
University School of Design**
Box 7701
200A Brooks Hall
Raleigh, NC 27695
(919) 515–8310
FAX (919) 515–7330

**Notre Dame University
Department of Art,
Art History & Design**
132 O'Shaughnessy Street
Notre Dame, IN 46556
(219) 631–7452
FAX (219) 631–6312

NYU Center for Digital Multimedia
719 Broadway
New York, NY 10003
(212) 998–3519

NYU Interactive Telecommunications Program
Tisch School of the Arts
721 Broadway #451
New York, NY 10003
(212) 998–1880
FAX (212) 998–1898

Ohio State University Department of Industrial Design
380 Hopkins Hall
128 North Oval Mall
Columbus, OH 43210
(614) 292–6746
FAX (614) 292–0217

Otis College of Art & Design
2401 Wilshire Boulevard
Los Angeles, CA 90057
(213) 251–0500
FAX (213) 480–0059

Parsons School of Design
66 Fifth Avenue
New York, NY 10011
(212) 229–8900
FAX (212) 929–2456

Pennsylvania State University School of Visual Arts
210 Patterson Building
University Park, PA 16802
(814) 865–0444
FAX (814) 865–1158

Pratt Institute School of Art & Design
200 Willoughby Avenue, PS 40
Brooklyn, NY 11205
(718) 636–3631
FAX (&18) 622–3553

Purdue University Division of Art & Design
1352 CA-1
West Lafayette, IN 47907
(317) 494–3058
FAX (317) 496–1198

Rhode Island School of Design
2 College Street
Providence, RI 02903
(401) 454–6100

Rochester Institute of Technology
College of Imaging
Arts & Sciences
73 Lomb Memorial Drive
Rochester, NY 14623
(716) 475–2634
FAX (716) 475–6447

**San Jose State University
School of Art & Design**
1 Washington Square
San Jose, CA 95192
(408) 924–4392
FAX (408) 924–4326

**Savannah College
of Art & Design**
Box 3146 Savannah, GA 31402
(912) 238–2400
FAX (912) 238–2456

School of Visual Arts
209 East 23rd Street
New York, NY 10010
(212) 679–7350
FAX (212) 592–2014

**Southern California Institute
of Architecture**
5454 Beethoven Street
Los Angeles, CA 90066
(310) 574–1123
FAX (310) 574–3801

**State University of New York
Purchase/Visual Arts
Department**
735 Anderson Hill Road
Purchase, NY 10577
(914) 251–6050
FAX (914) 251–6793

**Syracuse University
Department of Design**
334 Smith Hall
Syracuse, NY 13244
(315) 443–2455
FAX (315) 443–9688

UCLA Department of Design
University of California
1300 Dickson Art Center
Box 951456
Los Angeles, CA 90095
(310) 825–9007
FAX (310) 206–6676

**University of Advancing
Computer Technology**
4100 East Broadway #180
Phoenix, AZ 85040
FAX (602) 437–5695

University of the Arts
Broad & Pine Streets
Philadelphia, PA 19102
(215) 732–4832
FAX (215) 875–5458

**University of Bridgeport
College of Art & Humanities**
600 University Avenue
Bridgeport, CT 06601
(203) 576–4222
FAX (203) 576–4051

University of Cincinnati
College of Design
Cincinnati, OH 45221
(513) 556–0249
FAX 556–3288

University of Illinois
School of Art & Design
408 East Peabody Drive #143
Champaign, IL 61820
(217) 333–0855
FAX (217) 244–7688

University of Kansas
Department of Art & Design
Building #300
Lawrence, KS 66045
(913) 864–4401
FAX (913) 864–4404

University of Minnesota
Department of Graphic Design
Gunnar Swanson, head
Duluth, Minnesota

University of Washington
School of Art
Box 353440
Seattle, WA 98195
(206) 543–0970
FAX (206) 685–1657

University of
Wisconsin/Design Area
Milwaukee Department of Art
Box 413
Milwaukee, WI 53201
(414) 229–6934
FAX (414) 229–6154

University of Wisconsin
Stout Department of
Art & Design
324 Applied Arts
Menomonie, WI 54751
(715) 232–1141
FAX (715) 232–1669

Wentworth Institute
of Technology
Department of Interior &
Industrial Design
550 Huntington Avenue
Boston, MA 02115
(617) 442–9010
FAX (617) 442–3682

Yale School of
Architecture and Design
180 York Street
New Haven, CT 06520
(203) 432–4771
FAX (203) 432–7175

Brigham Young University
Design Department
210BRMB
Provo, UT 84602
(801) 378–2064
FAX (801) 378–2954

DESIGN ASSOCIATIONS / RELATED ORGANIZATIONS

**AIGA American Institute
of Graphic Arts**
164 Fifth Avenue
New York, NY 10010
(212) 807–1990
FAX (212) 807–1799

**American Association
of Advertising Agencies**
405 Lexington Avenue
18th floor
New York, NY 10174
(2120 682–8391
FAX (212) 682–8391

American Center for Design
325 West Huron Street #711
Chicago, IL 60610
(312) 787–2018
FAX (312) 649–9518

**American Institute
of Architects**
1735 New York Ave. NW
Washington, DC 20006
(202) 626–7568
FAX (202) 626–7426

**Art Directors Club
of New York**
250 Park Avenue South
New York, NY 10003
(212) 674–0500
FAX (212) 228–0849

**Association of Professional
Design Firms**
450 Irwin Street
San Francisco, CA 94107
(415) 626–9774

**Association of Graphic
Communications**
330 Seventh Avenue
New York, NY 10001
(212) 279–2100
FAX (212) 279–5381

Brand Design Association
164 Fifth Avenue
New York, NY 10010
(212) 807–1990
FAX (212) 807–1799

**Broadcast Designers
Association**
2029 Century Park E # 555
Los Angeles, CA 90067
(310) 712–0039
FAX (310) 712–0039

**Cooper-Hewitt National
Design Museum**
2 East 91st Street
New York, NY 10128-9990
(212) 849–8400
FAX (212) 849–8401

Corporate Design Foundation
20 Park Plaza #321
Boston, MA 02116
(617) 350–7097
FAX (617) 451–6355

Dallas Society of Visual Communications
3530 Highmesa Drive
Dallas, TX 75234
(972) 241–2017
FAX (972) 247–8735

Design Management Institute
29 Temple Place
Boston, MA 02111
(617) 338–6380
FAX (617) 338–6570

Graphics Communications Association
100 Daingerfield Road
Alexandria, VA 22314
(703) 519–8160
FAX (703) 548–2867

Graphic Artists Guild
90 John Street #403
New York, NY 10038
(212) 791–3400
FAX (212) 791–0333

Graphic Arts Technical Foundation
200 Deer Run Road
Sewickley, PA 15143-2600
(412) 741–2311

Graphic Design Educators Association
c/o University of Hawaii
College of Arts & Humanities
Dept. of Art
Honolulu, HI 96822
(808) 956–8251

International Association of Business Communicators
1 Hallide Plaza #600
San Francisco, CA 94102
(415) 433–3400
FAX (415) 362–8762

International Digital Imaging Association
84 Park Avenue
Flemington, NJ 08822
(908) 782–4635

International Council of Graphic Design Associations (ICONOGRADA)
P.O. Box 398
London, W11 4UH England
011-44-171-603-8494

International Design Conference at Aspen
P.O. Box 664
Aspen, CO 81612
(970) 925–2257

**International Society
of Graphic Designers**
Robert Linsky
201 Main Street
Charleston, MA 02129
(617) 241–7680

MDG.org Interactive Media
2601 Mariposa Street
San Francisco, CA 94110
(415) 553–2300
FAX (415) 553–2403

**National Association of
Schools of Art & Design**
11250 Roger Bacon Dr. Suite 21
Reston, VA 20190
(703) 437–0700

**National Endowment
for the Arts**
1100 Pennsylvania Ave. NW
Washington, DC 20506
(202) 682–5437
FAX (202) 682–5602

**OBD Organization
of Black Designers**
300 M Street SW #N110
Washington, DC 20024
(202) 659–3918
FAX (202) 488–3838

**Printing Industries
of America**
100 Daingerfield Road
Alexandria, VA 22314
(703) 519–8100
FAX (703) 548–3227

**SEGD Society
for Environmental
Graphic Design**
401 F Street NW #333
Washington, DC 20001
(202) 638–5555
FAX (202) 638–0891

**SGDC Society of Graphic
Designers of Canada**
National Secretariat
2 Daly Avenue
Ottawa, Ontario K1N 6E2
Canada
(613) 567–5400

**SMPS Society for Marketing
Professional Services**
99 Canal Center Plaza #250
Alexandria, VA 22314
(703) 549–6117
FAX (703) 549–2498

**Society of American
Graphic Artists**
32 Union Square #1214
New York, NY 10003
(212) 260–5706

Society of Illustrators
128 East 63rd Street
New York, NY 10021
(212) 838–2560

Society for News Design
129 Dyer Street
Providence, RI 02903
(401) 276–2100

**Society of Publication
Designers**
60 E. 42nd Street #721
New York, NY 10165
(212) 983–8585
FAX (212) 983–6043

Type Directors Club
60 East 42nd Street #721
New York, NY 10165
(212) 983–6042
FAX (212) 983–6043

**University & College
Designers Association**
122 South Michigan Avenue
Suite 1100
Chicago, IL 60603
(312) 431–0013
FAX (312) 431–9687

**Volunteer Lawyers
for the Arts**
1 East 53rd Street
6th Floor
New York, NY 10022
(212) 319–2787

DESIGN PUBLICATIONS

Communication Arts
410 Sherman Way
Anne Telford, Managing Editor
P.O. Box 10300
Palo Alto, CA 94303
(415) 326–6040

Critique
Marty Neumeier
120 Hawthorne Avenue
Palo Alto, CA 94301
(415) 323–7225

Design Issues
The MIT Press Journals
5 Cambridge Center
Cambridge, MA 02142
(617) 253–2889

Design Quarterly
Jensen & Wilcoxon Inc.
4411 Beard Ave. S.
Minneappolis, MN 55410
(612) 925–9150

Emigre
4475 D Street
Sacramento, CA 95819
(916) 451–4344

Eye
151 Rosebury Ave.
London ECIR 4QX England

Graphic Design USA
Kaye Publishing Corp.
Gordon Kaye, Editor
1556 Third Avenue #405
New York, NY 10128
(212) 534–5500

Graphis
Martin Pedersen, Publisher
141 Lexington Avenue
New York, NY 10016
(212) 532–9387

HOW Magazine
F&W Publications
Kathleen Reinmann, Editor
1507 Dana Avenue
Cincinnati, OH 45207
(513) 531–2222

ID Magazine
Chee Pearlman, Editor
440 Park Avenue S.
14th floor
New York, NY 10016
(212) 447–1400

Print
Joyce Rudder Kaye,
Managing Editor
104 Fifth Avenue
New York, NY 10011
(212) 463–0600

Step-by-Step Graphics
6000 N. Forest Park Drive
Peoria, IL 61614-3592
(800) 255–8800

U&lc
228 E. 45th Street 12th floor
New York, NY 10017
(212) 949–8072

Innovation
Industrial Designers
Society of America
1142 Walker Road
Great Falls, VA 22066
(703) 759–0100

@issue
Corporate Design Foundation
20 Park Plaza #321
Boston, MA 02116
(617) 350–7097

INDEX